FACE-TO-FACE
IN MANAGEMENT

DEREK TORRINGTON

University of Manchester
Institute of Science
and Technology

Prentice/Hall PHI International

ENGLEWOOD CLIFFS, NEW JERSEY · LONDON · NEW DELHI
SINGAPORE · SYDNEY · TOKYO · TORONTO · WELLINGTON

By the same author and also published by Prentice-Hall

PERSONNEL MANAGEMENT by D. Torrington and J. Chapman

British Library Cataloguing in Publication Data

Torrington, Derek
  Face to face in management.
  1. Personnel management
  I. Title
  658.3   HF5549

  ISBN 0-13-299099-7

ISBN 0-13-299099-7

PRENTICE-HALL INTERNATIONAL INC., London
PRENTICE-HALL OF AUSTRALIA PTY., LTD., Sydney
PRENTICE-HALL CANADA, INC., Toronto
PRENTICE-HALL OF INDIA PRIVATE LIMITED, New Delhi
PRENTICE-HALL OF JAPAN, INC., Tokyo
PRENTICE-HALL OF SOUTHEAST ASIA PTE., LTD., Singapore
PRENTICE-HALL INC., Englewood Cliffs, New Jersey
WHITEHALL BOOKS LIMITED, Wellington, New Zealand

Printed in Great Britain by A. Wheaton & Co. Ltd., Exeter

10 9 8 7 6 5 4 3 2 1

Contents

PART THREE   SPECIAL CASES AND CONCLUSION   181

Preface

In 1972 I published a slim volume entitled *Face to Face*, which set out a model for managers of four interactive encounters: selection, counselling, negotiation and addressing an audience. Each was presented in a simple sequence of preparation, encounter and follow-up. This has been a satisfactory book, remaining in print and still selling in different parts of the world. After acting as the basis of innumerable seminars and discussions, this same method of presenting interaction was used three years ago in the book *Personnel Management**, which had a recurring, integrative theme of the interactive encounter to be found at the heart of most activities of personnel managers.

This book extends the original face-to-face idea to eight different encounters, with the addition of more detailed general material at the beginning. The eight situations are not exclusive to the work of personnel managers and the writing tries to take account of the various ways in which the understanding of face-to-face encounters has developed in the last ten years.

Any merit which this book may have is enhanced by the illustrations that have been prepared by Sandra Ladley and Mark Windsor while they were students of management sciences at UMIST. I am indebted to Suzan Green for reading the manuscript and making many suggestions for improvement, and to Margaret Lees for typing so accurately and quickly. Most of all I acknowledge the assistance of hundreds of managers and management students who have helped, often unwittingly, to shape the material during the last decade.

Derek Torrington

Manchester, February 1982

*Torrington, D. and Chapman, J., *Personnel Management*, Prentice-Hall, London, 1979.

PART ONE

INTERACTION: THE BASIS OF MANAGEMENT

Chapter 1

Face-to-Face in Management

Talking with people is the main job that managers have to do: information is the stock in which they trade. In an organisation information is constantly being exchanged so that people know the little things, like the time to go home and how to get coffee, as well as the bigger things, like the job offer, the wage agreement, the reasons for dismissal, the prospects for promotion and the current state of the organisation's prosperity.

Conversation is so normal and universal that we do not always realise its importance. The most rapid surge forward in the development of our species came when the evolution of language enabled our forebears to exchange data and ideas, so that it became possible for the first time to plan; and the planning produced tools—and tools to make tools. Language also enables us to store information by providing a verbal code for ideas and images. It is most unusual for anyone to remember anything that happened to them before they personally learned to speak, as it is speech that encodes for storage in the memory (Schachtel, 1959). Despite its pervasiveness, few managers realise the amount of time they spend in conversation, and many feel that it is something which interferes with their "real" job. A number of studies have demonstrated this in the last thirty years (Stewart, 1970; Burns, 1954; Klemmer and Snyder, 1972, being among the best known). In 1973 Mintzberg showed a mean of 78% of working hours and 67% of working activities being devoted to interpersonal communication.

This degree of preoccupation has spawned much research and many books and courses about communication, interaction, human relations, interviewing, interactive skills, organisation behaviour, information networks, information flow, transactional analysis, body language, non-verbal behaviour, gestures, kinesics, proxemics, interpersonal behaviour, self-presentation, impression management, management meetings, sensitivity training, small-group behaviour, counselling and so on.

This book concentrates on various types of face-to-face encounter undertaken by those doing managerial work. The approach is first to examine interaction as the central feature of managerial work, and to describe various aspects of *method* in handling face-to-face situations. These will mainly be aspects of understanding other people and getting messages across to others. Secondly there is a discussion of typical face-to-face *situations*, with suggested ways of handling them.

1.1 The Changing Context of Face-to-Face Encounters

The main interest in this topic for managers is their obvious wish to improve effectiveness in communication, but there are certain features of current development in organisational life that give the subject particular significance.

1.1.1 Employee Participation

There is a tendency and a growing need to increase the amount of employee participation in traditionally managerial aspects of organisational affairs. This can take many forms, with industrial democracy in terms of control of the decision-*making* process being one of the less likely and least common. More widespread is the need to involve non-managerial employees in the effective *implementation* of decisions. This is one of the ways in which managers are less able to depend on the straightforward exercise of authority or power, as the jobs to be done in organisations become more skilled. This makes managers more dependent on the employee's skill and training, together with his understanding of the varied organisational requirements that the manager is trying to coordinate.

The easiest example of this is the work of the account director in an advertising agency, where the copywriter, the artist, the photographer and others all have to be brought to share the same vision of what they are together going to produce. The contribution that each can make has to be understood by the account director and the vision of what is possible from the group will develop through the consultative process. With the increasing variety of organisational tasks, employee contribution cannot often be *commanded* in the sense that a manager knows what is to be done, the employee does not, the manager instructs him, the employee complies precisely and then waits for further orders. Sometimes the contribution can be *specified* by a manager deploying an employee with a known set of skills who is required to use his skill and knowledge to achieve a stated objective ("repair that machine" or "check this building for fire hazards"). More and more the contribution has to be *devised* while it is explained, interpreted, justified, modified and "won" as the manager constantly blends the work of various people in getting decisions implemented and, perhaps, in the decision-making process itself. Both require more talking.

1.1.2 Matrix Patterns of Organisation

A development closely allied to the argument of the last two paragraphs is that of the matrix organisation. This has been most accurately described recently by Charles Handy (1976 and 1978). In the matrix employees have two types of role identification within the organisation; one to their functional specialism and one to a task group. A television make-up artist, for example, will be part of the grouping of make-up specialists in the company, but will mostly be deployed on a particular assignment, where the affiliation will not be to a team of make-up experts, but to a group of people, led by a producer, involved in making a programme.

Many employees of complex organisations spend their working lives in a series of task groups like this, so that they participate full-time in one project for a few weeks or months before being reassigned to a different project. For the team leader, and the team members, this presents the need to adjust their social style constantly to a fresh group of semi-strangers. They all have autonomous expertise, but it is only their collaborative efforts that will bring achievement. This mixture of autonomy and interdependence has to be orchestrated by the manager.

1.1.3 The Professionalisation of Interaction

A third aspect of the changing context is the tendency to professionalise the work involved in interpersonal exchanges. The semi-permanent selection interviewer has been a feature of organisational life for many years, but more recently we have seen the appointment of professional counsellors, negotiators and change agents, as well as advisors on virtually every topic known to man. Professional arbitrators and mediators may still be very rare, but there are many people who are already cornering their companies' markets in grievance – hearing and discipline – handling. We have market research interviewers, trade instructors and lecturers; and the twin activities of management development and performance appraisal enable some people to make an art out of assessment interviewing.

Professionalising a job always produces a range of insider techniques to justify the profession. It is declared as being special and sufficiently unique for people to do nothing else. In that case there has to be a magic component to justify the specialisation. This is usually some esoteric knowledge or developed skill. Professionalising interaction has specialised the skills of interaction. The selector specialises in selection and the negotiator specialises in negotiation: simple fluency or "being good at communication" is no longer enough.

There are other important aspects of context, like the growth and expansion of education, the search by employees for a wider degree of personal fulfilment at work and so forth, but the need for participation, the matrix form of organisation and the move to professionalisation are features not usually recognised as having particular significance to the subject matter of this book.

1.2 Growing Understanding of Face-to-Face Encounters

We come to know more about interactions almost daily, as various studies are published. Unfortunately, more knowledge does not always mean better understanding, as the studies tend to diverge rather than converge, but there are three main areas of study and explanation.

1.2.1 Psychologists

By far the biggest volume of work in the area has been by psychologists and psychiatrists, with their focus on the individual and the small group. One approach is epitomised in the work of Michael Argyle, working at Oxford, who has produced an excellent review of the field in *The Psychology of Interpersonal Behaviour* (1972) as well as the more scholarly *Social Interaction* (1969). He has carried out extensive experiments himself and draws on a number of other fields of study in his approach, explaining interaction in terms of the range of elements that comprise human behaviour.

Another development linked to training is *sensitivity training* which develops the awareness that participants have of themselves, their effects on other people and the ways in which small groups operate. The best account of this technique is by Bunker (1965). A follow-on is the work of the American psychiatrist Eric Berne, who analysed relationships between people as game-playing and then evolved a form of therapy he called *transactional analysis*. Both Berne and Argyle lay emphasis on the way in which emotional states and intentions are signalled by non-verbal behaviours, which has become a beguiling area of popular study.

1.2.2 Social Anthropologists

It is sometimes difficult to discern the difference between sociology and social anthropology, but essentially social anthropology is that develop-

FTFIM - B

ment within the science of anthropology that is a search for origins and the study of different societal traditions. The change came as a response to the new discipline of sociology in the nineteenth century and caused the *social* anthropologist to study contemporary social life and to analyse the constitution of societies. One of the main contributions from this area to our understanding of interaction is the study of *ritual*. Once we begin to appreciate the place of ritual in all forms of social exchange, then we come to an understanding of some of those aspects of interaction which appear so irrational and obstructive. Whenever aspirants for professional/managerial/administrative posts attend employment interviews they present themselves in a way that seeks to conform to a stereotype:

> . . . well-washed and quietly-dressed . . . politely attentive, submissive, and keen . . . He may need to show what a decisive and forceful person he is—but without using those powers on the selection board. (Argyle, 1972, pp. 201–202)

This is not because all those who sit on selection panels believe it important to be able to wear a pin-stripe suit, but because there is an appropriate ritual for the employment interview and the applicant who broke from the ritual behaviour would feel insecure. One anthropologist has claimed

> Rituals reveal values at their deepest level . . . men express in ritual what moves them most, and since the form of expression is conventionalised and obligatory, it is the values of the group that are revealed. I see in the study of rituals the key to an understanding of the essential constitution of human societies. (Wilson, 1954)

If ritual is a profound aspect of our behaviour, we cannot dismiss it, as so many managers do, as being "mere" ritual that should be ignored or eliminated in order to get on with what really matters. Hundreds of elements in interactions exist primarily or partially for ritualistic reasons.

One of the great contributors from the sociological/social anthropological background towards better understanding of interaction is Erving Goffman. His work is never less than riveting and his most absorbing book (1969) contains an analysis of interaction in terms of the performances that people present to others. He argues that all of us are constantly seeking information from each other that is not readily revealed, so that we infer it from a range of cues, like gesture. At the same time we are deceiving those trying to obtain the same sort of information from us by the art of *impression management*, through which we try to create impressions of ourselves that are more favourable than the facts warrant. He also describes the way in which behaviour alters between what he calls the "front" regions of workplaces and "backstage". Just as actors present one sort of performance on the stage and behave quite differently as soon as they are out of public view, so Goffman describes exactly the same behaviour by all people at work. Negotiators manage the impression they are creating while negotiations are in progress, but as soon as there is an adjournment the impression management is relaxed and exchanges are more informal and revealing of true feelings.

Some anthropological ideas have been taken up enthusiastically by management writers. Two books in the 1970s (Cleverly, 1971; Jay, 1975) concentrated on organisational structures and managerial behaviour, using anthropological ideas as a basis. Cleverly examines management as magic, explaining much managerial behaviour as ritual and especially taboos. The value of his work for this book is his description of how information and opinion are evaluated in terms of their source as well as their content:

> No matter how carefully calculated, exhaustively analysed, and voluminously documented, a project presented by someone without the requisite magical attributes invites rejection. But the same project presented by a man with an established reputation for executive virility is likely to be accepted if it is, figuratively speaking, written on the back of an envelope. (Cleverly, 1971, p. 213)

1.2.3 Zoologists

A surprising influence on interaction has come from the more popular aspects of the work of a series of zoologists (some better described as ethologists) who have come to conclusions about human behaviour as a result of studying the animal world and then making the logical step that man is an animal and therefore similar. Lorenz (1966) and Ardrey (1969) produced explanations of aggression and territorial protection that were to prove influential on popular opinion, and helped to modify folklore in organisations about the effect, for instance, of the interviewer's desk on the attitude of an interviewee. More recently Desmond Morris has produced a series of books stripping away some of the concealing layers of human behaviour to reveal the "naked ape" beneath. His most important work in the context of interaction is a natural history of gestures (Morris, 1977) that complements that of some psychologists studying non-verbal behaviour.

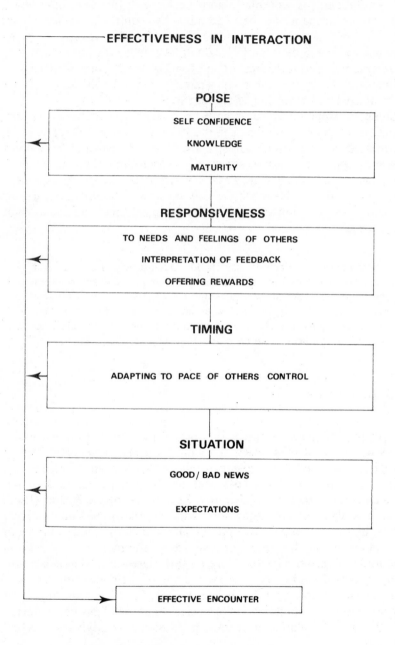

Fig. 1.1 Effectiveness in interaction.

1.3 Effectiveness in Interaction

With the growing understanding of the interaction processes it is possible to develop greater effectiveness in the way people handle encounters. This is the purpose of this book and will be the subject of the remaining chapters, but it is appropriate here to mention some of the general factors that contribute to one person being usually effective while another is less effective.

1.3.1 Poise

The skilled interactor is at ease in a wide variety of social situations, often enjoys them, and is able to talk with different types of people in a relaxed and self-confident way. This self-confidence derives in part from the feedback constantly received confirming the willing response that others make. This is not to be confused with a style that is overbearing at one extreme, or unctuous and ingratiating at the other. Many people seek to dominate interactions by talking loudly or at length without being at ease and usually convey a sense of unease to the other participants in the conversation.

Another element of poise and self-confidence is the substantive feature of knowing what it is you are talking about, so that we demonstrate our poise much more in situations with which we are familiar than we do in strange circumstances. There is less fear of what the other may say and less apprehension about appearing naïve. Questions, and even criticism, are easier to deal with and are often wanted, so stimulating the interchange. There is almost certainly a minority of people whose behaviour contradicts the norm in that they thrive on, and actively seek, the challenge of uncertainty in which they put together a performance which is not only an inaccurate representation but which derives its effectiveness from the stimulus of living dangerously.

Poise is traditionally associated with maturity, due to a person having succeeded in developing a rounded view of themselves without too much anxiety about the possible adverse opinions of others. This can be accelerated by experience, where the experience involves meeting a wide variety of people from differing backgrounds, particularly where one is dependent on those people.

1.3.2 Responsiveness

The first necessary adjunct to poise is the quality of being responsive t the needs, feelings and level of understanding in other participants in the interaction. This is what prevents the poise from becoming too ego-centric. At the cognitive level this will involve being responsive to the degree of "the other's" understanding.

The teacher, for instance, will be looking for signs of misunderstanding in the student so that the message can be restated or clarified, and the market research interviewer will be looking for signals that his question has been accurately construed, or whether it needs elaboration.

At another level there will be responsiveness to the emotional state of the other. The training of dentists used to include "watching the dial", which was the process of the dentist observing the face of the patient while drilling holes in his teeth. When the patient winced, the dentist would ease the drill away from the nerve that was being macerated. Inter-actors do not usually inflict physical pain in quite the same way, but they will be on the look-out for signs of physical discomfort in those with whom they are speaking. "Can you hear?", "Can you see?", "Are you in a draught?", "Is the sun in your eyes?" are all questions to which answers will be sought, even though the answer may be inferred by some aspect of the other's behaviour rather than as a spoken response to a spoken question.

Responsiveness can also include offering rewards, like friendliness, warmth, sympathy and helpfulness as features of general style or as part of a relationship with other participants. These not only sustain and strengthen the relationship, they may also be held back as a means of manipulation in trying to get one's own way.

1.3.3 Timing

Much of human artistry in performance depends on timing. This is most obvious in the physical arts like dance, gymnastics and ball games, but is also a requirement of any vocal performance. The operatic duet, the cross-talk comedy act or any stage play, all depend upon the skill with which the performers time their exchanges. The exchanges which are the subject of this book also depend on timing, without the complication of an audience as a third party. Skill is required first in adapting to the inter-active methods of others and then taking control to move into a smooth and efficient rate of exchange. The other person may be verbose or tongue-tied, bright or dull, bombastic or diffident. The skilled interactor uses his poise and responsiveness to "pick up" the rhythm of the other and either adjust himself to that or adjust both rhythms to what provides the basis for an exchange that is both comfortable and efficient. A helpful analogy is learning to play tennis, where the tyro is absolutely dependent upon the person at the other side of the net. The skilled player will help the learner by playing back the ball in a way that the learner can cope with, largely being consistent, and gradually sharpens the game by speeding up the exchanges.

Timing difficulties occur when one party tries to override or interrupt the other because of impatience, or where there are misunderstandings and awkward silences in the exchange. They can also be caused by lack of social skill or by a phase in the interaction which presents particular problems or anxieties to one of the parties.

1.3.4 The Situation

In many instances the situation surrounding the exchange is the overriding consideration. If you have to tell someone that they are to be dismissed, the style and the context of the exchange will both be important. If you have to tell someone that they have passed their examinations, the gladness of the tidings make the subtleties of interaction irrelevant. This is much complicated by the expectations we all have. The opening gambit of, "Come in and sit down, John. There is something I want to talk to you about", tends to signal bad news, and if you have bad news to deliver it is most infuriating when you signal it in behaviour and *then* laboriously prepare the ground in what you say before you deliver the message.

1.4 Problems in Interaction

The remaining chapters of this book take a close look at face-to-face communication, but there are certain general problems that can impair effectiveness. They are mostly aspects of the way in which people tend to hear what they expect to hear.

1.4.1 The Frame of Reference

This is the standpoint from which a person views an issue, and perceptions of the issue will be shaped by that perspective rather than an abstract "reality". A transaction, for instance, is seen quite differently according to whether you are buying or selling. It is not, however, simply a question of the role that is being played in the situation; in sociological terms the frame of reference is a set of basic assumptions or standards that determines and sanctions behaviour. These assumptions are developed through childhood conditioning, through social background, education and affiliations, and it is the differences in the frames of references held by participants in interaction that is one of the inescapable problems. Can the Russians and the Americans ever really understand each other? How can those who manage and direct ever appreciate the point of view of those who are managed and directed?

The frame of reference on a particular matter is largely determined by opinions developed within a group with which we identify, as few of us alter our opinions alone. We both follow and participate in the formulation of opinion in our group, and most of us are in a number of such reference groups. This produces complexities: some people can be vociferously anti-union as citizens, members of their local community and voters in general elections, yet support a union of which they are members at their workplace.

A manager who is trying to persuade someone to change their behaviour or attitude to work may have to struggle with the fact that the values informing the behaviour of the person he is talking to are different from his own, may not alter, or may move only when the values of his reference group alter. Both participants in the interaction will "see reason", but the reason they see will be different.

1.4.2 The Stereotype

The stereotype is the standardised expectation we have of those who have certain dominant characteristics: all women are catty, all Scots are mean, all shop stewards are disruptive, all mathematicians are poor in using words. The behaviour of some people in a category makes us expect all people in that category to behave in the same way. This is obviously invalid, but is a tendency to which we are prone so that we are likely to hear someone say what we *expect* them to say rather than what they *do* say. At first this is necessary in interaction; it is not feasible to deal with every individual we meet as being a void until we have collected enough information to know how to treat him. We begin conversations with a working stereotype, so that we stop someone in the street to ask directions only after we have selected a person who looks intelligent and sympathetic. If we are giving directions to a stranger we begin our explanation having made an assessment of their ability to understand quickly, or their need for a more detailed, painstaking explanation. The stereotype becomes a handicap only when we remain insensitive to new information enabling us to make a rational appraisal of the individual with whom we are interacting.

Being aware of the dangers of stereotyping others, and trying to exercise self-discipline, can reduce the degree of false understanding of other people that stereotyping can cause, but you still have the problem that your respondents will put *you* into a stereotype and hear what you say in accordance with whatever that predetermined notion may be.

1.4.3 Cognitive Dissonance

This describes the difficulty we all have in coping with behaviour that is not consistent with our beliefs. This will make us uncomfortable and we will try to cope with the dissonance in various ways in order to reduce the discomfort. Either we persuade ourselves that we believe in what we are doing, or we avoid the necessary behaviour. When we are given new information that is not consistent with what we already believe, we are likely to massage it to fit our existing pattern of behaviour rather than jettison the beliefs of a lifetime. One example of this is the many stories that circulate about the arrival of the computer in the office. It was explained very carefully to Fred that it was no longer necessary for him to keep detailed ledger records as the computer would do that for him; all he had to do was to make the decisions. Fred nodded eagerly, for we seldom acknowledge that there is a dissonance in our cognitions, but three weeks later the night watchman came across him at three in the morning secretly bringing his ledger up to date. Cognitive dissonance makes it hard for us to understand new information, harder to believe in it and hardest of all to take any action based upon it.

1.5 The Importance of Interaction

The importance of interaction lies in its function of making things happen in organisational life. However detailed the application form and however elaborate the tests, it is the interview which determines whether a potential employee joins the organisation or not. Promotion, performance appraisal and overcoming problems at work similarly depend upon discussion and exchange, as does training, negotiating agreements, selling products, terminating contracts and so on. These relatively formal exchanges are in addition to the thousands of minute-by-minute conversations that encourage, reassure, explain, advise, rebuke and inform. A useful summary is

1. In the pursuit of their work goals, people have forces acting upon them to communicate with those who will help them achieve their aims, and forces against communicating with those who will not assist, or may retard their accomplishment.
2. People have powerful forces acting upon them to direct their communication toward those who can make them feel more secure and gratify their needs, and away from those who threaten them, make them feel anxious and generally provide unrewarding experiences.
3. Persons in an organisation are always communicating as if they were trying to improve their position. (Jackson, 1959)

The manager in the organisation is the person who is constantly enabling these types of interaction to take place and conducting them himself. Interacting is a skill and this book is intended to help people enhance their skill in this most pervasive of managerial activities.

References

Ardrey, R., *The Territorial Imperative*, Collins, London, 1969.

Argyle, M., *Social Interaction*, Methuen, London, 1969.

Argyle, M., *The Psychology of Interpersonal Behaviour*, Penguin, London, 1972.

Berne, E., *Games People Play: Psychology of Human Relationships*, Andre Deutsch, London, 1966.

Berne, E., *What Do You Say After You Say Hello?*, Andre Deutsch, London, 1972.

Bunker, D. R., "The effects of laboratory education on individual behaviour", in Schein, E. H. and Bennis, W. G., *Personal Learning and Organisational Change through Group Methods*, John Wiley, New York, 1965.

Burns, T., "The directions of activity and communications in a departmental executive group", in Porter, L. W. and Roberts, K. H., *Communication in Organizations*, Penguin, London, 1977.

Cleverly, G., *Managers and Magic*, Longman, London, 1971.

Goffman, E., *The Presentation of Self in Everyday Life*, Penguin, London, 1969.

Handy, C. B., *Understanding Organisations*, Penguin, London, 1976.

Handy, C. B., *Gods of Management*, Souvenir Press, London, 1978.

Jackson, J. M., "The organisation and its communication problems", in Porter, L. W. and Roberts, K. H., *op. cit.*

Jay, A., *Corporation Man*, Penguin, London, 1975.

Klemmer, E. T. and Snyder, F. W., "Measurement of time spent communicating", in Porter, L. W. and Roberts, K. H., *op. cit.*

Lorenz, K., *On Aggression*, Methuen, London, 1966.

Mintzberg, H., *The Nature of Managerial Work*, Harper & Row, New York, 1973.

Morris, D., *Manwatching*, Jonathan Cape, London, 1977.

Stewart, R., *Managers and Their Jobs*, Pan/Piper, London, 1970.

Wilson, M., quoted in Sutherland, A., *Face Values*, BBC Publications, London, 1978.

Chapter 2

Understanding People by Watching Them

In every conversation you have the other person is lying to you. The lies are usually white lies, but they still obscure the truth. Often it is in minor, unimportant ways. If someone says, "Hello, how are you today", the reply will usually be along the lines of, "Fine, thanks. How are you?", no matter what the true state of mind or health that the other is experiencing. We make varying degrees of effort to appear interested when cornered by a bore: only an extraordinary person would decline conversation by saying, "No, I do not wish to talk with you because you are invariably excruciatingly boring".

Sometimes the lie can be important. The trainee may say he understands when in fact he does not, because he believes that admitting to misunderstanding will make him foolish or even get him into disfavour. The candidate in a selection interview will frequently be less than candid for fear of losing the job offer. In a number of situations managers are told by employees what they "want" to hear rather than what they need to hear. Man is a dissembler. This is both a feature of *manners*, that require us to refrain from certain types of frankness, and an aspect of how we manipulate situations or *manage* the impressions we convey to others. There is always the temptation to find out what the other person is *really* thinking by getting behind the words and seeing the "truth" in involuntary gestures, signs and cues that signal an attitude or an emotional condition that is contradicted by accompanying words.

This is a dangerous temptation as the evidence that can be gained from these non-verbal cues is unreliable. Folding arms does not always indicate aggression and soft, wet, flabby handshakes do not invariably mean that the other person is of low moral fibre. *You* avoid giving that impression by remembering to wipe the palm of your hand on the seat of your trousers and then shaking hands firmly. Perhaps *he* has done the same thing and tricked you.

Even though prediction is unrealiable, an awareness of the research in this area can give additional inklings of what other people might mean and feel. This understanding can also help us in the way we convey meaning to others.

2.1 The Study of Non-verbal Communication

The first investigation of non-verbal communication was in the work by Charles Darwin, *The Expression of the Emotions in Man and Animals*, which was published in 1872. The search for explanations in the behaviour of animals *and* man is also a feature of the recent past, with a number of people studying and reflecting upon behaviour in its natural state. The leading contemporary exponent of this form of analysis is Morris (1977, 1979) although earlier writing by Lorenz (1952, 1966) and Ardrey (1969, 1977) provide insights that are particularly relevant to instinctive behaviour.

Different from the natural history approach is that of the social psychologist, whose contribution has lain in the activity of controlled experiment and the testing of hypotheses. Founding father, Freud, made the comment in 1905:

> . . . no mortal can keep a secret. If his lips are silent he chatters with his finger tips, betrayal oozes out of him at every pore.

Apart from one somewhat isolated early work by Efron (1941) the great expansion in the body of literature came in the 1950s. Birdwhistell (1971, 1973) coined the term *kinesics* to describe the study of human communication by means of body movement and proceeded to analyse movements on film with the most painstaking diligence in setting up a vocabulary of *kinemes*, which are fragments of behaviour that produce an unvarying response in the observer. After some criticism, Birdwhistell acknowledged that the meaning of body signals varied according to context, but he makes a convincing case that certain facial expressions can be accurately read in almost any situation.

Another contribution from this period was the work of an anthropologist, Hall (1959), who also coined a new word—*proxemics*—to describe the way in which space is used as a form of communication. Basically we move closer towards those we like and trust, but away from those we fear or dislike. Hall identified four zones around each individual:

Intimate zone (0–½ metre). This is only viable when there is an intimate relationship with the other person or when the two are fighting. Touch and smell are important means of communication, as it is difficult to see clearly. Words can be whispered.

Personal zone (½–1½ metres). The two people must be well acquainted to feel comfortable, although they do not have to be intimate. Conversation is likely to be hushed.

Social zone (1½–3½ metres). This is the zone in which most business behaviour takes place, as befits the impersonal relationship between, say, salesmen and client.

Public zone (3½ metres +). At this range strangers do not exist as individuals and can be comfortably ignored. If there is to be interaction words have to be delivered loudly, as on public occasions.

Fig. 2.1 The four zones of communication: intimate, personal, social and public.

This period also saw the emergence of Goffman (1968), as was mentioned in the previous chapter, and Hewes (1957) who made an anthropological study of posture. Argyle's first publication on this subject came in 1957 and other contributors to an understanding of the area have been mainly Scheflen (1972), Mehrabian (1972), Ekman (1967) and Ekman *et al.* (1971).

2.2 The Background to Non-verbal Communication

Understanding others by looking at them is an art with a long history of folklore and half truths. Consider how Hamlet interpreted a simple picture of his father:

> See what grace was seated on this brow;
> Hyperion's curls; the front of Jove himself;
> An eye like Mars, to threaten and command;
> A station like the herald Mercury
> New lighted on a heaven-kissing hill –
> A combination and a form indeed
> Where every god did seem to set his seal,
> To give the world assurance of a man.

Apart from the general impression that is conveyed, is there a sort of eye that can threaten and command, so that when you see it you know how to respond? It is a superb image, but of doubtful practical value. Equally dubious are ideas like the weak chin, the strong face, the stiff upper lip and numerous other nostrums attributing an aspect of character to a physical signal.

Among the early attempts to codify these meanings was the invention of *physiognomy* by Aristotle. He observed that each animal has a special predominant instinct, so that the fox is cunning and the wolf ferocious. He then argued that men with features resembling a particular animal would have qualities similar to the animal. The idea fascinated the French and German painters Lebrun and Tischbein in the seventeenth and eighteenth centuries before finding its best-known advocate in Johannes Lavater. In 1775 he published a four-volume work setting out a system for reading the character in a face from its lines and contours. Although he became a celebrity and gained enthusiastic adherents as diverse as Goethe and Catherine the Great, his system was not soundly based, so that physiognomy now has no more credibility than phrenology or palmistry. Its weakness is demonstrated by the fact that Lavater describes a profile that almost exactly duplicates his own as

> The countenance of the hero: active, removed both from hasty rashness and cold delay. Born to govern. May be cruel but scarcely can remain unnoticed.

We will still see sensitive faces, soulful eyes and determined chins, but we can only make these judgements erratically and on the basis of personal experience.

A similar marginal note in the development of understanding is the series of experiments carried out by Sheldon (1954) at Harvard. He set out to classify human beings according to their body, or *somatype*, by putting the relationship between physique and behaviour on a scientific basis. We can again turn to Shakespeare for illustrations of the folklore, as Falstaff was fat *and* jolly. Cassius thought too much and was dangerous, and Caesar knew that because of his lean and hungry look. After exhaustive analysis Sheldon produced the following groupings:

> *Endomorphs* have soft rounded bodies, weak in bone and muscle structure. They are generally sociable, pleasure-loving, relaxed and good sleepers.
>
> *Mesomorphs* are hard and muscular and likely to be aggressive, callous, athletic and dominating.
>
> *Ectomorphs* are tall, thin and fragile. They are self-conscious, solitary and intense, probably sleeping badly.

This categorisation tends to confirm what we all instinctively believe despite notable exceptions. Mussolini was obviously an endomorph, but

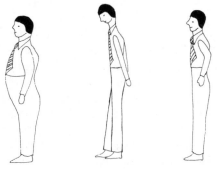

Fig. 2.2 Sheldon's three somatypes: endomorph, mesomorph and ectomorph.

behaved like a mesomorph; Picasso was a mesomorph who should have been an ectomorph. The relationship between body type and behaviour is more subtle than Sheldon implied, but there can be little doubt that the general expectation that people have of the behaviour of others will follow the pattern he suggests. One wonders whether there is any significance in the fact that Sheldon's father was an animal breeder! We must also note that his work was on classifying the body types of adult *males*.

The greatest degree of uncertainty in interpreting the behaviour and intention of others by looking at them is the effect of *culture*. There is, for instance, marked variation in the degree of physical contact that is made in different societies. In the Middle East the European visitor is surprised to see young men walking along the street hand-in-hand, which would be less acceptable behaviour in Manchester. Leaders of the USSR greet visiting dignitaries by kissing on both cheeks: behaviour most unlikely in their American counterparts. Ekman, Ellsworth and Friesen (1971) tested the universality of facial expression meanings by showing photographs of university students to aborigines and asked for judgements about the feelings that were being expressed. The aborigines then posed for photographs that were shown to American students.

Although the two sets of judgements were not perfect, there was a high degree of correlation suggesting that the following emotional states may be shown by universally recognisable facial expressions:

anger, disgust, fear, interest, joy, sadness, surprise.

The researchers also observed that it was much more difficult for someone to judge the *intensity* of emotion in a person of a different culture. It is easy to tell that he is angry, but how angry? This element of universality is not surprising when we appreciate that some components of facial expression are very difficult to control, like perspiring, blushing, trembling and goose pimples. Other ways we reveal our feelings are easier to control and therefore more variable from one culture to another. The recent work of Morris has been largely concerned with this type of variation in gesture, for example:

> ... there is a simple gesture in which the forefinger taps the side of the nose. In England most people interpret this as meaning secrecy or conspiracy ... 'Keep it dark, don't spread it around,' but as one moves down across Europe to Central Italy, the dominant meaning changes to become a helpful warning: 'Take care, there is danger — they are crafty'. The two messages are related, because they are both concerned with cunning. In England it is *we* who are cunning, by not divulging our secret. But in Central Italy it is *they* who are cunning, and we must be warned against them. (Morris, 1977, p. 53)

2.3 The Main Signals

Now we move on to review some of the principal ways in which the feelings and intentions of others can be inferred from an aspect of their behaviour.

2.3.1 The Use of Space

We move closer to those we like or in whom we have confidence, and move away from those we fear or distrust. The wary and apprehensive candidate at a selection interview will tend to distance himself from the interviewer, perhaps even unthinkingly moving the chair slightly backwards before sitting down. If he develops confidence and becomes less wary, then the orientation would gradually shift towards the interviewer.

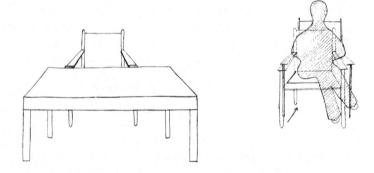

Fig. 2.3   The moving chair of the diffident assistant.

A powerful senior manager may want to work through some documentation with an assistant, so he tells him to "pull up a chair and look at this". The assistant, who is diffident (perhaps because he wrote the report that is being scrutinised) will either move his chair to a relatively distant position so that he can only see by leaning forward uncomfortably and unnaturally, or he will vacate his chair and go to stand where he can see. He has the comfortably-distant chair to retreat to at the earliest possible moment.

Space also involves territory. One reason why the assistant does not want to get too close to his superior is because the superior's desk and chair have territorial-defensive indicators all over them to assert his

Fig. 2.4 Territorial paraphernalia.

ownership. There is the velvet cushion his wife made last winter, the studio photographs of the children, the personalised keyring attached to the key in the lock of the private drawer, the desk set, the blotter with his own doodlings in the top right hand corner, his pipe, his glasses, his diary and all the paraphernalia that says to other people: "This is mine; keep off".

There are all manner of ways in which this territory is protected and used in organisational life. Open-plan offices are full of rubber plants and filing cabinets that are gradually shifted, nudged and rearranged until each occupant of the office has marked out his own territory and put mini walls round it. Waiting rooms and lifts provide daily examples of territory definition. The first person in the waiting room will take up the best strategic position – back to the wall, able to see the door, not likely to be overlooked. The next best position is logically the adjoining chair, but that is one place that will *not* be occupied by the next person to come into the room. When people enter a lift there is a clear sequence. The first person takes up a position just inside the door, near the controls. The second person goes to the diametrically opposite corner. When a third enters he will stand in one of the two remaining corners, and numbers one and two will both squeeze themselves more firmly into the corners they have already occupied. Number four takes up the last corner and number five has no choice but to stand, vulnerable, in the middle. As more enter there are desperate attempts by everyone to avoid touching if at all possible and eyes are fixed intently on the indicator of which floor the lift has reached. Nobody speaks and all seem almost to be holding their breath until the doors open and someone gets out to relieve the tension.

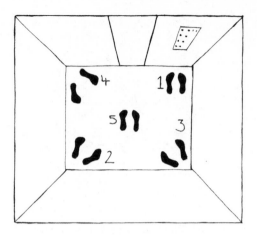

Fig. 2.5   Positions in the lift.

Scheflen (1972) gives useful advice on how to select conversations to break in on at receptions and buffets. If two people are talking while facing each other directly, they would not welcome interruption; if they are at an angle of 90° to each other they are probably hoping to be interrupted, and if the angle is any greater they are pleading for help!

This is echoed in the conclusions of Sommer (1969) and Cook (1970), both of whom demonstrated a relationship between positioning around tables and the nature of the interaction. Those preparing to compete, negotiate or argue sat at opposite sides of a table, while those expecting to cooperate were more likely to sit side by side. The preferred position for conversation was for the parties to sit at a 90° angle.

Fig. 2.6   Which pair do you join?

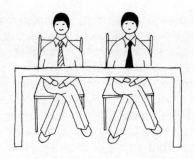

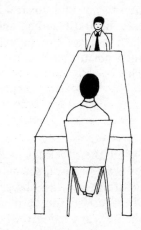

Fig. 2.7 Seating and the nature of the interaction.

Morris describes how territory can be protected in a public library. A pile of books on a table effectively reserved the chair adjacent to the books for 77 minutes, and a jacket over the back of the chair extended the reservation period to 120 minutes (Morris, 1977, p. 132).

The value of understanding some of these signals is to be able both to identify them and manipulate the situations in which they occur. If a factory manager is about to conduct some negotiations in his office with a group of shop stewards it would not be helpful to arrange the furniture as if for a friendly, brainstorming type of meeting. The negotiating nature of the encounter is best reflected in opposed, "them and us" seating arrangements. A counselling interview will involve building a degree of mutual confidence that may be difficult to achieve across a desk, but much helped by a 90° orientation.

The observant selection interviewer will not produce questions that the applicant might find threatening until he has noticed the applicant giving some of the small signals to indicate growing trust and confidence: various aspects of the applicant's posture will move towards the interviewer rather than pulling back.

2.3.2 Posture

Most people realise that they show their feelings in their faces, but few realise that they also do this in their posture, so there is less likelihood that posture will be controlled to prevent the observer picking up any clues. For this reason it can be a useful source of information. In an argument, for instance, someone may unwittingly signal defeat by allowing his shoulders to slump while continuing to be defiant in his language.

Height is a significant aspect of posture. Tallness tends to make one person physically dominate another and relative shortness is seen as a disadvantage for which the short seek compensation by aggressiveness, volubility or some other dominant characteristic. Women are normally shorter than men and have been wearing much higher heels for a very long time to even up that difference. Public speakers stand on a rostrum or in a pulpit. When Anna went to be a governess in the Siamese court she was much inconvenienced – and later millions of cinema-goers were much amused – because no head could be higher than that of the king, even if the king was lounging on the floor. A fictional Spanish grandee placed all his self-esteem in the fact that he enjoyed the rare privilege of being allowed to wear his hat in the presence of the king.

In organisational life we emphasise or de-emphasise our height according to our perception of a situation. If a foreman feels that he has to assert himself with a member of his department he will tend to pull his head up and back. The salesman leaving a meeting with a client who has indicated that he will probably place an order will tend to duck his head as he leaves and bow slightly when shaking hands.

Mehrabian (1972) has explained some posturing according to what he calls the "immediacy principle", similar to the proximity principle described above. Immediacy behaviours are leaning forward, touching, getting close, looking straight at the other and orienting directly. All improve mutual visibility and reduce the distance between the two people, so that some of these behaviours will be displayed by the person who is drawn to, confident in, or friendly towards, the other. If our feelings about the interaction are negative, then we will tend to pull back, lean back, turn our head away, break eye contact and depart as soon as possible.

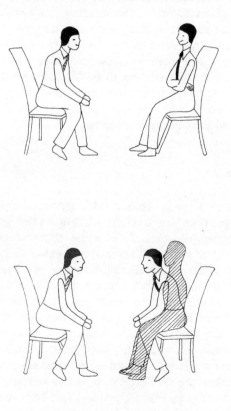

Fig. 2.8 Postural echo.

An interesting feature of posturing is what has been called the postural echo, whereby one person automatically adopts the general posture of the other, or adopts one particular feature of that collection of postures. One person begins to tell a story while leaning forward in his chair, knees apart, elbows on knees, hands loosely clasped. As soon as the other person's interest is engaged he leans forward in his chair, links his hands and rests his elbows on parted knees. This is a signal of friendship and support that is made instinctively. In organisational life skilled interactors use their understanding of this to manipulate interactions. A personnel officer who has to conduct a disciplinary interview which involves trying to understand why an employee is not acquiring the necessary degree of speed and accuracy on an initial training programme, may find that the trainee comes and sits quietly, hands on lap, looking at the floor. If the personnel officer then also sits down quietly and echoes the other postural components he will get in tune with the employee more readily than by standing at the window with arms crossed. Another example is judging the mood of a meeting, where two contrasted points of view are being expressed. The non-committed will gradually echo the postures of those whose point of view they find most persuasive. Also their posture may change as their mind changes, so that they signal a growing uncertainty by dropping a postural echo. The highly observant chairman can thus decide the appropriate time to take a vote or to express a view that should gain general consent.

2.3.3 Gesture

Investigators have devoted considerable energy to interpretation of gesture. Some gestures are obvious and universal in their meaning. Beckoning, for example, means the same thing wherever it is used. General emphasis, or underlining, is found extensively in gesture, and the meaning is again unequivocal—banging on the table or other behaviour that accompanies and directly relates to what is being said.

Hewes (1973) has suggested that gesture preceded language as a means of communication among primitive men and that we retain the remains of a gesture language to accompany our speech, so that we are able to make ourselves understood with relative ease on most matters when amongst foreigners with whom we have no common language, just as we can understand the subtleties of meaning contained in the mime of Charlie Chaplin or Marcel Marceau. It has also been suggested (Baxter *et al.*, 1968) that more gestures are used in the conversation of those with high verbal facility than by those without, so that gesture supplements speech rather than substitutes for it.

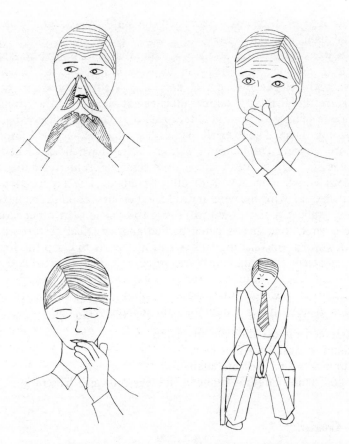

Fig. 2.9 Four of Krout's "autistic gestures": steepled fingers, hand to nose, fingers to lips and hand dangling between legs.

Because of the connection between gesture and language there is also a strong connection between gesture and culture, so that it seems quaint to Western eyes when a Russian leader responds to applause from his followers by clapping himself. This is another aspect of non-verbal behaviour where Morris shows the range of variations.

Gesture is used to synchronise verbal exchanges. The opening chapter mentioned the importance of timing and the skilled interactor will be deft in synchronising what he has to say with what the other has to say. This is mainly done by language and gaze, but is supported by gesture. The person seeing the other about to speak when he himself has not finished will not only talk louder and more quickly, he is also likely to look directly at the other, possibly raising his eyebrows, and may produce a blocking gesture towards the other by raising his hand, with the palm *down*. If that same person is seeking a response from the other and wants to signal him in, then his gesture will be similar but more relaxed and with the palm *up*.

Gestures that reveal something about a person involuntarily are difficult to decode. Shivering can indicate either cold or nervousness because both trigger the central nervous system to produce the same physical result. Rubbing palms indicates anticipation while rubbing the back of one's hands indicates cold. Shrugging shoulders shows disinterest and waving means "good-bye". Much less obvious and well known are the more obscure *displacement activities* that have been identified by physiologists. When in a state of stress we sometimes engage in behaviour which is irrelevant or out of context. The prospective father waiting anxiously for his wife to produce their first child in the next room typically walks up and down to relieve the tension. In other situations people scratch their heads when baffled and a typical gesture – particularly in women – in reacting to news of a crisis is to clasp the forehead. To some extent smoking can be regarded as a displacement activity.

Krout (1954) conducted a series of experiments to identify what he called *autistic gestures*, that were involuntary indicators of specific attitudes. Among his less obvious conclusions were that:

> steepled fingers indicate suspicion,
> hand to nose indicates fear,
> fingers to lips indicate shame, and
> open hand dangling between the legs indicates frustration.

2.3.4 Gaze

As with gesture, gaze is a component of synchronising in interaction, so that we look at the other twice as much while he is talking than while he is listening to us. In talking we look away more in order to both collect our thoughts and to spare the other the uncomfortable experience of being looked at while inactive. If we are wanting to signal the other into the conversation ("nearly finished what I'm saying; your turn coming up . . .") we will wind up our contribution by accompanying our closing words with a period of looking at the other directly, with slightly raised eyebrows. The exchange of looks forms a strong bond between people. The waiter in the restaurant may ignore you for a long period, but once you have "caught his eye" then he is drawn towards you, however reluctantly. The important manager arriving in the office is at pains to acknowledge everyone he passes on the way to his sanctum. A nod, a half-smile, a wave; whatever the signal it is accompanied by a brief instant of eye contact to recognise and acknowledge. If he does not do that but marches purposefully in, looking neither to the right nor the left, then shock waves move rapidly round the building.

Generally the direction of gaze is a device for keeping the other "in play". The public speaker will sweep his audience with his gaze from time to time to maintain the bond. If he fails to do this and fixes his eyes on his notes or a corner of the ceiling, then the audience will tend to lose concentration. In a different way the same principle applies in one-to-one encounters. The counsellor looks at his client to signal attention and understanding, and to provide feedback. If he does not look at the client, the client will talk with less precision; if he looks at the client too much, the client will be inhibited. Forbes and Jackson (1980) showed that gaze is one of the more telling aspects of non-verbal behaviour for applicants in selection interviews. They studied various aspects of the ways in which school-leavers behaved in applications for apprenticeships. Those applicants who produced more smiling, eye contact, head nodding and head shaking than average improved their chances of being offered a job. Variations in body position were not found to have any effect on selectors' decisions. The behaviours which produced the favourable effect on interviewers were, of course, all ways of showing interest.

2.3.5 Bodily Contact

A very specialised method of communicating is by physical contact. A pat on the back is both physically and metaphorically a way of encouraging. Less common in business life are spanking and stroking, although their verbal equivalents are extensively used. The great message-sender is the handshake, to which passing reference has already been made. Folklore decrees that a firm, dry handshake comes from someone with a strong character and reliable personality, while a limp, moist handshake comes from someone who is weak and untrustworthy. This was illustrated in one of the volumes of reminiscences of Edward Heath (1977, p. 31). He describes how he met Goebbels and Himmler while he was a member of a student group touring Germany before the Second World War:

> Himmler received us all, peering rather shortsightedly through his pince-nez. I remember him for his soft, wet, flabby handshake. Goebbels was there, his pinched face white and sweating – evil personified.

At the close of the war Edward Heath was serving with the British forces in Germany:

In 1945 I heard the BBC announce the death of Himmler. 'There he
lay', said the reporter, 'and they threw a blanket over his dead body'.
His words had a strange but simple nobility about them. My mind
went back to that flabby handshake in Nuremberg. That plain piece
of English prose was far more than he deserved.

The deeds of Himmler – particularly in 1945 – were widely known and
execrated, yet what immediately came into Edward Heath's mind, and
what was still there thirty years later when he wrote the book, was a
single handshake. Five minutes' tuition could have turned even Himmler
into an exponent of the firm, dry grip, yet conventional wisdom still says
that character can be judged from this momentary contact; partly because
this is the only exchange of this type that we ever have. There are handshake variations that can be deployed to indicate greater degrees of
warmth and reassurance, or dominance. The first is to hold on for a
longer period. If that is accompanied by a vigorous pumping action it
conveys enthusiasm for the meeting. The other main variant is the use of
the left hand. This may be added to the basic hand-to-hand clasp, or may
take hold of the other's forearm, elbow or shoulder. All of these convey
friendliness, plus an edge of superiority and initiative-taking in the
relationship. An important qualification that must be attached to this
particular signal is that the folklore categorises firm handshakes as
indicators of strong character only in men, as it is traditionally mainly a
male activity.

2.3.6 Miscellaneous Aspects of Non-verbal Behaviour

The way we dress and groom our personal appearance contains a set of
signals about how we want to be appraised by others, particularly the
social grouping with which we identify. There are a number of uniforms
for different occupational groups; the clearest examples being barristers,
who always wear formal black jacket and trousers with a white shirt.
Sales representatives have a norm of charcoal grey suiting, white shirt
and executive brief case. As the need for occupational security through
attachment to a group decreases, so the grooming becomes more personal
and idiosyncratic. Potter (1970, p. 177), provides a nice satirical
comment on professional uniforms by showing the Hampshire general
practitioner in top hat and frock coat while the President of the Royal
College of Physicians wears an old fishing jacket.

Frequently, people in conversation use artifacts as ways of gaining
time for thought. Most common are pipes and spectacles. If the pipe-

smoker is asked a question and wants to take time to reply without giving the impression that he *needs* time, he may relight his pipe or plunge a dead match into one of its noisome recesses for a second or two. The spectacle-wearer may put them on to look at something, or he may suddenly realise that he can't find them, so that a short space of time can be won by busily patting pockets and peering myopically under pieces of paper scattered about the desk. Other ploys are fishing a handkerchief out from pocket or handbag, being overtaken by a slight fit of coughing, or simply moving from one position in the chair to another.

Finally, the importance of non-verbal behaviour is demonstrated by the fact that it is more cogent than speech. Actions literally speak louder than words, and when they conflict the action wins. A popular party game for children involves a leader giving instructions, with gestures, for the children to follow. Occasionally the instruction and the accompanying gesture conflict and all those who followed the gesture rather than the words drop out. This game will usually last for five or ten minutes. If the rules are reversed so that players drop out when they obey the gesture rather than the words, there is such a low failure rate that the game lasts twice as long! The interviewer who signals inattention or impatience by shuffling papers and drumming fingers on the table will find that this signal overrides his words that are asking what he can do to help.

References

Ardrey, R. *The Territorial Imperative*, Collins, London, 1969.

Ardrey, R. *Hunting Hypotheses*, Fontana, London, 1977.

Argyle, M. *The Scientific Study of Social Behaviour*, Methuen, London, 1957.

Baxter, J. C., Winter, E. P. and Hammer, R. E., "Gestural behaviour during a brief interview as a function of cognitive variables", *Journal of Personality and Social Psychology*, **8**, 303–307 (1968).

Birdwhistell, R. L., *Introduction to Kinesics*, Penguin, London, 1971.

Birdwhistell, R. L., *Kinesics and Context*, Penguin, London, 1973.

Cook, M., "Experiments in orientation and proxemics", *Human Relations*, **23**, 61–76 (1970).

Efron, D., *Gesture and Environment*, King's Crown Press, New York, 1941.

Ekman, P., "A methodological discussion of nonverbal behaviour", *Journal of Psychology*, **53**, 141–149 (1967).

Ekman, P., Ellsworth, P. and Friesen, W. V., *Emotion in the Human Face: Guidelines for Research and Integration of the Findings*, Pergamon Press, New York, 1971.

Forbes, R. J. and Jackson, P. R., "Non-verbal behaviour and the outcome of selection interviews", *Journal of Occupational Psychology*, **53**, 65–71 (1980).

Hall, E. T., *The Silent Language*, Doubleday, New York, 1959.

Heath, E. R. G., *Travels – People and Places in my Life*, Sidgwick & Jackson, London, 1977.

Hewes, G. W., "The anthropology of posture", *Scientific American*, **196**, 123–132 (1973).

Krout, M. H., "An experiment attempt to determine the significance of unconscious manual symbolic movements", *Journal of General Psychology*, **51**, 121–152 (1954)

Lorenz, K., *King Solomon's Ring*, Methuen, London, 1952.

Lorenz, K., *On Aggression*, Methuen, London, 1966.

Mehrabian, A., *Nonverbal Communication*, Aldine Atherton, Chicago, 1972.

Morris, D., *Manwatching*, Jonathan Cape, London, 1977.

Morris, D., *Gestures*, Stein & Day, London, 1979.

Potter, S., *The Complete Upmanship*, Rupert Hart-Davis, London, 1970.

Scheflen, A. E., *Body Language and Social Order*, Prentice-Hall, Englewood Cliffs, NJ, 1972.

Sheldon, W. H., *Atlas of Men: A Guide to Somatyping the Adult Male at all Ages*, Harper & Row, New York, 1954.

Sommer, R., *Personal Space*, Prentice-Hall, Englewood Cliffs, NJ, 1969.

Chapter 3

Getting Your
Message Across

In getting your message across to others you have to work on what *they* hear from you and understand: not on what you say. The politician who says in a television interview,"I would like to make it perfectly clear . . ." may be doing more to clarify his thoughts to himself than convey an accurate message to his audience. This makes it important for the inter-actor to concentrate on *feedback* and *listening*, as this is how he can test the accuracy of the picture being put together in the mind of the other as a result of his transmitted signals. A well tried way of illustrating this is to use the analogy of telecommunications.

3.1 The Communications Model

Figure 3.1 shows that a person with an abstract idea that he wants to get across begins by *encoding* it. The idea is translated into speech patterns or actions to substitute for, or embellish, what is to be said. The signal is then *transmitted* by the words or actions being produced. The receiver picks up the message with some or all of his senses and *decodes* it. That decoding is not a simple mechanical process but an interpretation, and the code book used is that of the receiver's personal experience, expecta-tion, trust, initial level of understanding and all the other factors that make for individual difference in perception. It is clearly in the encoding/decoding process that error will occur. The sender of the message will try to use a code that is appropriate to the receiver who will decode the message in its context, by taking into account what he knows about the sender before he starts to unscramble the signal. After decoding there is the final loop that closes the circuit of communication: *feedback*. The receiver gives some indication to the transmitter that he has received the message, and the nature of his response will usually indicate something of the quality of his understanding.

Communication is therefore both mutual and circular and feedback offers the opportunity for correction or reshaping of the original message. The sender has the opportunity to add to or alter his original message in order to clarify it and the receiver has the opportunity of testing his decoding to make sure he has registered the message that the sender intended.

An example might be the thirsty man approaching a bar. He encodes his thought by saying, "A glass of beer, please". His preoccupation with his own thirst is such that he provides little information apart from the bare necessity of beer. The bartender has little initial difficulty as he

COMMUNICATION MODEL

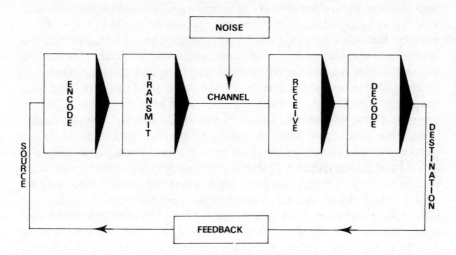

Fig. 3.1   The communications model.

expects people to come into his bar asking for beer. It is only the person asking for a glass of water who might be required to repeat the question. However, he has different sizes of glass and different types of beer, so he has a choice of responses that will provide his feedback. He may know the customer and add the necessary details himself, so that the initial message is shown to be adequate. He may receive the message in the context of a sender who looks as if any type of beer in any type of glass will do, so he pours out his own choice which the customer drinks; again showing the initial message to be adequate. A further possibility is that he indicates to the customer the inadequacy of the message by looking puzzled, and this type of feedback enables the sender of the initial message to add information, like "A half pint of bitter" which will lead to the feedback loop being completed by the barman pouring what is required. A fourth possibility is for the receiver to shape the message by providing feedback that specifies his difficulties in decoding, like ". . . pint or half . . . mild or bitter . . .?"

A final component of the communications process is "noise". That is anything that interferes with the quality of the message transmitted and received. We are all familiar with the experience of tuning a radio set to a signal in such a way as to avoid the "static" which obscures the weak signal if we have a poor receiver or have not tuned in correctly. In face-to-face communication the idea of noise can be used to cover all manner of things from the obvious problem of making yourself heard and understood above the sound of the pneumatic drill in the road outside, to the less obvious minor distractions of inattention, a familiar perfume that you cannot quite identify or wondering where he bought those shoes.

To transmit effectively we have to *listen* carefully, because of the mutual and circular process that communication comprises. We have to be on the look-out for signals and willing to spend the time needed to listen and build understanding, deliberately holding back our own thoughts, which would divert or compete with the other. This is unusual. If you eavesdrop on conversations, you usually hear two people competing with each other to speak rather than to listen. They are putting on a display, using the other person rather like a punch-bag. The careful and patient listener is able to build on what the other is saying by planting his own ideas in the seed bed of what the other is interested in, or concerned about, and able to understand. Another aspect of listening is the ability to extract the real message from all the mass of material that is expressed. This has been called "listening with the third ear" (Reik, 1948) and is almost the opposite of the example of the man in the bar who provided too little information. Many people provide too much, largely by being bound up with their own preoccupations, and the third ear enables the listener to pick out the significant elements and to discard the remainder.

We sometimes underestimate the amount of time we spend listening. Maude (1977) cites studies showing that dieticians spend up to 63% of the time listening and 22% talking, while adult employees generally spend 42% of their time listening and 32% talking. For such a time-consuming activity it behoves us to do it as skilfully and effectively as we can.

We now move to consider specific aspects of method in communication by setting out a number of *ploys*, or ways in which the interactor can best get himself understood or understand what he wants to know. They are grouped into five categories – opening, questioning, feedback, closing and general – and are placed at this stage in the book because they are to be found in a number of interactive incidents that are described later: this chapter should be a resource chapter for the remainder of the book. Certain of the more specialised ploys used in, for instance, lecturing and negotiating are dealt with in the specialised chapters that follow.

3.2 Opening Ploys

Interactions usually open with a degree of skirmishing as each party assesses the other and tunes in. This is sometimes called "bonding" or "verbal togetherness" (Malinowski, 1923) and is followed by more subtle behaviours to support the relationship and maintain the credibility of the attitudes that were demonstrated at the beginning.

3.2.1 Rapport:
Enabling the participants to interact effectively

This is a common behaviour, which most people undertake quite instinctively a dozen times a day. "Hello, how are you today?". "Can't complain. How are you?" "Not so bad for the time of year, I suppose. Be better by five o'clock". "Ha, won't we all! Well, see you later". "Right, cheers". That type of ritual conversation takes place on staircases and in changing rooms regularly, and the same pair of people will say the same things to each other day after day, but they have bonded at the beginning of a new day and the fact that their exchange is always the same has a certain reassurance about it. In interviews and committees, however, there is greater formality in the exchanges which make this stage of the proceedings more important than in casual encounters, especially when strangers are meeting for the first time, as in most employment interviews and much selling.

All parties to the encounter will have an interest in setting up rapport, but in the more formal situations there will be a duty on the clear controlling figure—the selection interviewer, the counsellor, the tutor etc.—to take the initiative. Here are some of the standard methods.

(a) Small talk
The staple component is small talk that does not matter in substance. Most common is the weather or the temperature, so that the participants can use an innocuous topic to exchange words and sounds with each other while they adjust to each other's tone and volume and assess the other's personality, beginning to relax in the presence of their counterpart.

(b) Friendly, easy manner
This is so much easier to advocate than to produce. In many of the situations we explore later in this book the person not directing the interaction will be wary or ill at ease. It will nearly always help the conduct of the encounter itself if that suspicion is allayed, so that he speaks more fully and frankly. The first step is to show friendliness in the opening display, but that will have to register with the receiver as friendliness and not as condescension, falseness or casual indifference. This is difficult to do and most problems occur with people who try too hard and come across as insincere.

(c) Calm attention

The interviewer who is able to project a feeling of peacefulness and quiet will elicit a response from the other person more quickly and constructively than the interviewer who deliberately or unwittingly conveys an atmosphere of busyness and preoccupation. If the interviewer can create an unhurried atmosphere he will complete the encounter more quickly than if he underlines the fact that he can only spare a few minutes. Paying attention to what is being said will focus the thinking and responsiveness of the other person.

(d) Explaining the procedure

In any interaction the respondent will be uncertain about what is to happen, because of his dependence on the other to direct proceedings. The interviewer can build rapport by explaining aspects of the procedures. Who he – the interviewer – is, and the part he plays in the process; how long the conversation is likely to take and what the interviewer would like to accomplish are useful here. If the respondent is to take an initiative at any stage, this is usefully signalled during rapport: ". . . there will obviously be questions that you want to ask, and there will be plenty of time for that later on". Now that he knows the protocol, he can think of one or two matters to raise, as he feels that he is *expected* to ask questions, and will lose points if he does not.

3.2.2 Reward:
Sustaining the smooth pattern of interaction with the respondent

Rapport, obviously, is set up at the beginning of the encounter, and does not take too long and become laboured. After a very few minutes the conversation will move to the substance that the two people have come together to discuss. It is important, however, that the interviewer does not leave behind the warm and responsive behaviour that he displayed at the beginning: that has to be maintained throughout the encounter. We need to ensure that establishing rapport is not mechanical, but a ritual that is used to make the interaction work. Examples of falseness in rapport exchanges are the health service administrator who opened each selection interview with a question about the candidate's journey. As each reply came in one of the normal variations of "Very nice, thank you", he reacted with a standard, hearty "Splendid!" Unfortunately the exchanges became so mechanical that he produced the same "Splendid!" when one candidate told him that he had had a puncture and arrived ten minutes late. An earnest interviewer of school-leavers applying for jobs in a well known bank always exchanged pleasantries for three minutes with a strained smile before changing his expression to one of pained disapproval and saying, "Well, I think we've established rapport, so I will proceed with the questions". Rapport has to be kept going throughout the encounter. Some of the conventional methods are given here.

(a) Interest
We all respond positively when a listener is interested in what we are saying, so the interested interviewer will encourage and draw out the respondent by his interest. If he can also demonstrate that he *agrees* with what is being said, his reinforcement of the respondent will be greater.

(b) Affirmation
A talker is always looking for the reaction of the listener in order to complete the feedback loop in the communication circuit, and the reaction he needs is affirmation. The most common form is the head nod, and many public speakers look for head nods as a way of judging the supportive mood of the audience. Other ways of affirming are the use of the eyes. These are too subtle and individual to describe, but we each have a repertoire of signals to indicate such reactions as encouragement, surprise and understanding. When the eyes are part of a smile, there will be stronger reward to the talker. There are also words and phrases, "Really?", "Go on . . .", "Yes . . . ", "Of course . . .", "My word . . .", "You were saying . . .". All the while the affirmations keep coming, the talker will be fluent, but if the responses lapse he will tend to stumble and hesitate.

(c) Noises
Conversation contains a variety of noises that are ways of rewarding the other party. They are impossible to reproduce in words but are usually variations of a theme of "Mmm . . ." and they form a part of the conversation that is inarticulate yet meaningful, and keep things going without being interruptions.

(d) Silence
An episode of silence in a conversation is usually seen as a lull, that must be filled. Someone must say something, anything, to fill the dreadful void of silence. However, most of the encounters described later in this book are formal conversations in which silence may be necessary, while someone processes a new thought. A question posed in performance appraisal, for instance, may be greeted with initial silence. The unwise interviewer will feel that he has discomfited the respondent and will fill

the silence by suggesting the answer, or rewording the question, when in fact the silence is needed for the respondent to collect his thoughts to provide a considered answer. Mayerson (1979) suggests that thirty seconds is not too long to leave a silence:

> . . . it is more helpful at first to let the silence happen. There is a temptation to fill it up as if it were an empty basket. This has negative effects, especially if the silence is a productive one or one of great feeling . . . The length of time one should let silence alone is arbitrary. It depends on the cues one is getting and one's own comfort with the situation. A very general rule of thumb is 30 seconds. That is a long time. More than 30 seconds lets everyone forget what was happening, and takes the participants away from the emphasis of the subject.

3.2.3 Exploding:
Bringing latent, suppressed feelings into the open

This last, melodramatically named ploy is for use in those specialised situations where there is some pent up feeling that the interviewer believes should be expressed early in order to clear the way for subsequent discussion. It is a ploy that is used in discipline or grievance settlement on occasions, but is less common in other encounters.

(a) Letting off steam
As with the above comment on silence, this requires the interviewer to do what might not be natural and easy. Many managers ignore signals of frustration in respondents because they do not want to get into a difficult or contentious situation, and the warning signals are disregarded. If, however, a respondent is showing obvious signs of anger or distress at the start of an encounter, it can be helpful to encourage the blow-up and the rush of feeling that follows. It will not solve the problem, but it will at least make the rest of the conversation more constructive.

(b) Digging
Sometimes the anxiety or disappointment in the respondent is latent, but not pent up to the extent that the lid will blow off the head of steam. There may still be the need to bring the disquiet to the surface in an attempt to prevent further festering. The signals are harder to read and will probably only be seen by someone who knows the respondent well, who may then try a sally like, "There seems to be something on your mind?"

3.3 Questioning Ploys

Most interactions contain questioning and some of the main types of question can be classified.

3.3.1 Closed Questions:
Questions seeking precise, terse information

When we want precise, factual information we close the question to control the answer:

> "Is it Mrs or Miss?"
> "Who is in charge?"

These are useful questions when it is unvarnished data that is being gathered and most encounters have some feature of closed questioning.

3.3.2 Open-ended Questions:
Questions avoiding terse replies, and inviting the respondent to develop his opinions

Here the respondent is enabled to speak without having the interviewer prescribe his answers. The question does little more than introduce a topic to talk about:

> "How are you getting on?"
> "What does your present job entail?"
> "What are your future plans?"

Open-ended questions often come at the beginning of an encounter as a means of developing the rapport. It makes things easy for the respondent, giving him latitude to decide what to talk about and helping him to relax and get going. Their main purpose, however, is to obtain information, but the information obtained is not that which can be predetermined by the questioner.

3.3.3 Direct Questions:
Questions "insisting" on a reply

Now the interviewer is asserting his authority and his "right to know".

The direct question uses the prescriptive *style* of the closed question but is seeking fuller information of the type that open-ended questions usually deliver, unless the respondent is being evasive:

"Did you take the money?"
"Why did you leave that job?"
"Did you, or did you not, clock Charlie Miller in yesterday?"

3.3.4 Indirect Questions:
Questions taking an oblique approach on a difficult matter

These are questions with the same general objective as direct questions but taking an indirect approach. Higham (1979, p. 134) gives an example of how an indirect question can be a more effective approach than the direct alternative:

> 'What were your colleagues like in that job?' is preferable to 'Did you get on all right with the rest of the office?' But the virtues of the indirect question go further still. A blunt 'Did you like that job?' almost suggests you didn't, or at least raises the suspicion that the interviewer thinks you didn't! Put indirectly as 'What gave you the most satisfaction in that job?', it has the merit of concentrating on the work rather than the person . . .

3.3.5 Probes:
Questioning to obtain information that the respondent is trying to conceal

This is not so much a style of questioning as a tactical sequence to deal with those situations in which the supportive and encouraging interviewer can be deflected by a respondent who is not to be cajoled, by the winning ways of reward and open-ended questions, into divulging information that he is anxious to conceal.

When this happens the interviewer has to make an important, and perhaps difficult decision: does he respect the respondent's unwillingness and let the matter rest, or does he persist with his enquiry. Reluctance is quite common in disciplinary and grievance interviews, where someone may be reluctant to criticise a colleague, and in employment interviews there may be an aspect of the recent employment history that the candidate wishes to gloss over. The most common sequence for the probe takes the following form.

(a) Direct questions
Open-ended questions give too much latitude to the respondent, so direct
questioning is needed. Careful phrasing may avoid a defensive reply.

(b) Supplementaries
If the first direct question produces only evasion, then a supplementary
will be needed, reiterating the first with different phrasing.

(c) Closing
If the probe is used when the rapport is well established, it stands the
best chance of being successful, but it then needs to be closed skilfully. If
the information has been wrenched out like a bad tooth and the interviewer looks horrified or sits in stunned silence, then the respondent will
feel himself put down beyond redemption. The interviewer needs to
make the divulged secret less awful than the respondent had feared, so
that the encounter can proceed with reasonable confidence. For example:

> "Yes, well you must be glad to have that behind you".

There is a dirty trick that can be used as an alternative method of
probing. Although no reader of this book would ever dream of using this
tactic, it is described below so that he can see it coming if anyone does it
to him.

(d) Overstatement
If a suggestion is put to the respondent implying a reason for his reluctance that is more grave than the real reason, then he will rush to correct
the false impression.

> Q. "There appears to be a gap in the employment history at the
> beginning of last year. You weren't in prison or anything, were
> you?"
> A. "Good heavens, no. I was having treatment for . . . er . . . well,
> for alcoholism, actually".

A thoroughly dirty trick, but effective.

3.3.6 Proposing Question:
A question used to put forward an idea

This is a question for feeling a way out of an impasse, and is to be found
in negotiation, brainstorming and other situations where there is
difficulty in pulling people together. It is a ploy to test for consensus

without being sufficiently positive to be an assertion which then has to be defended:

"Well, now that we have the consultant's report we must clearly accept Jim's earlier suggestion".

The second is the tactic of the acknowledged leader in a group, or it is a bid for leadership by one member challenging the rest to disagree.

3.3.7 Rhetorical Question:
A question "forbidding" a reply

This is really a way of making a statement, as it poses a question in such a way that the answer is too obvious to state. Replying to a mixture of allegations about incompetent behaviour, a manager might ask:

"How can we be slack on purchasing procedures and too strict on reorder levels, both at the same time?"

3.4 Feedback Ploys

There are two ploys to be mentioned under this general heading, even though some of the main behaviours have already been described in rapport and reward.

3.4.1 Summary and Re-run:
Drawing together in summary various points from
the respondent and obtaining his confirmation

The respondent will produce lots of information in an interview and the interviewer will be selecting that which he wishes to retain and understand. From time to time he will interject a summary sentence or two with an interrogative inflection:

"You did take the wallet out of his locker, then, but this was because he had asked you to fetch it for him so that he could repay Charlie his fiver?"

"So the difficulty in meeting the sales target has been more to do with production problems than with customer demand?"

This tactic serves several useful purposes. It shows the interviewer is listening and gives the respondent the chance to correct any false impressions. It also reinforces the key points that are being retained and is a useful way of making progress, as the interjection is easily followed by another open-ended question – "Now perhaps we can turn to . . .".

3.4.2 Reflection:
Turning the respondent's comment back to him so that he says more on the same topic

When a respondent makes a comment that has more in it than appears on the surface it is "reflected". Beveridge (1968) provides an excellent summary of its use in counselling situations:

> . . . a selective form of listening in which the listener picks out the emotional overtones of a statement and 'reflects' these back to the respondent without any attempt to evaluate them. This means that the interviewer expresses neither approval nor disapproval, neither sympathy nor condemnation. Because the respondent may be in an emotional state, sympathy is liable to make him resentful or angry. Any attempt to get the respondent to look objectively and rationally at his problem at this stage is also likely to fail; he is still too confused and upset to be able to do this and will interpret the very attempt as criticism.

Mayerson (1979b) describes a similar tactic as *empathic feedback*. An example of how this would be done is in the following exchange:

Respondent: "Seniority does not count for as much as it should in this company".

Reflection: "You feel there is not enough acknowledgement of loyalty and long service?"

Alternative reactions would have a different effect, for example:

"You sound like someone who has been passed over for promotion", or
"Oh, I don't know about that".

Both push the respondent on to the defensive, so that he has to justify his position against manifest disagreement or disapproval, and he may not say what was in his mind. Another alternative:

"Well, I think seniority has been overemphasised in the past", stifles the opinion before it has been fully expressed. The respondent who is diffident will not develop his feeling, so the matter cannot be resolved. There is also the danger that any one of these evaluative reactions could evoke a comeback from the respondent which complies with the view suggested by the interviewer. This is the same problem as that of the leading question, which is dealt with shortly.

3.5 Braking and Closing Ploys

So far the respondent has been mainly encouraged by the interviewer, but it is easy to nod and smile your way into a situation in which the respondent has relaxed to a point where he talks on and on . . . and on. Also, there are a surprising number of interviewers who can begin an interview smoothly but have great difficulty closing, so there are two ploys to suggest.

3.5.1 Braking:
Slowing the rate of talking by the respondent

It may be necessary or appropriate to become peevish with the overtalkative respondent, but braking provides a sequence of less drastic techniques. You will seldom need to go beyond the first two or three, but five are offered in case of you having to deal with a really tough case, like a university lecturer or an insurance salesman.

(a) Closed questions
It has already been pointed out that the closed question invites a terse response. One or two closed questions interjected to clarify specific points may stem the tide.

(b) Facial expression
The brow is furrowed to indicate mild disagreement, lack of understanding or professional anxiety. The reassuring nods stop and the generally encouraging, supportive behaviours of *reward* are withdrawn.

(c) Abstraction
The respondent may not notice the facial expression points mentioned above, so the next step is for the eyes to glaze over, showing that they

belong to a person whose attention has now shifted away from the respondent and towards lunch or last night's football match.

(d) Looking away

To look at one's watch during a conversation is a very strong signal indeed, as it clearly indicates that time is running out. Most people are very reluctant to do it and often an interviewer will take his watch off before the interview and put it in front of him where he can look at it discreetly. You, however, may prefer to keep it on your wrist so that you can look at it more obviously and so slow down a verbose respondent. Other milder ways of looking away are: looking for matches or glasses, looking at your notes or looking at the aircraft making a noise outside the window. A rather brutal variant is to allow your attention to be caught by something the respondent is wearing – a lapel badge, a tie, a ring or piece of jewellery, maybe. Putting on your glasses to see it more clearly is really rather unsportsmanlike!

(e) Interruption

The most blunt of methods. Most people avoid it at all costs, but in the end you have no choice.

3.5.2 Closing:
Finishing the interview without "losing" the respondent

In closing an interview future action is either clarified or confirmed. Also the respondent takes a collection of attitudes away with him, and these can be influenced by the way the encounter is closed, particularly after counselling or disciplinary interviews. There is a simple procedure:

(a) First signal, verbal plus papers

The interviewer uses a phrase to indicate that he regards the interview as nearing its end:

> "Well now, I think we have covered the ground, don't you?"
> "I don't think there is anything more I want to ask you. Is there anything further you want from me?"

In this way he is signalling the impending close and at the same time obtaining the respondent's confirmation. There is additional emphasis provided by some paper play. A small collection of notes can be gathered together and stacked neatly, or a notebook can be closed.

(b) Second signal, explaining the next step
The interviewer confirms what will happen next:

> "Can we meet again next week, to see how things are proceeding?"
> "There are still one or two people to see, but we will write to you no later than the end of the week".

(c) Closing signal, stand up
As the ground has been prepared, all that is now required is the decisive act to make the close. By standing up the interviewer forces the respondent to stand as well and there remains only the odds and ends of handshakes and parting smiles.

3.6 Pitfalls

Some common behaviours can produce an effect that is different from what is intended:

3.6.1 Leading Questions:
Questions that suggest what the "correct" answer should be

They will not necessarily produce an answer which is informative, what they *will* produce is an answer in line with the lead that has been given.

> "Would you agree with me that . . ."
> "I believe in strict control of expenditure and firm handling of debtors: what about you?"

Unless you want a sycophantic response, or are really using the question rhetorically, leaders are of little value, and can be misleading in the replies they produce.

3.6.2 Unreasonable Exhortation:
Expecting a change in emotional state as a result of complying with an instruction

This is a commonplace which does more for he who exhorts than for he who is exhorted because the change that is sought is rarely a simple matter of will:

"Stop crying".
"Relax".
"Cheer up".

3.6.3 Multiple Questions:
Questions that give the respondent too many inputs at one time

This is sometimes found in interviewers who are trying very hard to efface themselves and let the respondent get on with the talking, so there is an occasional attempt to put a number of questions together. The idea is that the respondent can then use them as a stock to draw on when he is ready:

"Well can you just tell me why Fred threw the spanner at you, if it really was Fred, what you did when you saw it on the floor and what on earth the start of all this silly horseplay was?"

3.6.4 Taboo Questions:
Questions that infringe the reasonable personal privacy of the respondent

Although there is a proper place for the probe, there are some questions that have to be avoided, usually in selection interviews, as they could be interpreted as discriminatory. It is at least potentially discriminatory in selection, for instance, to ask women how many children they have and what their husbands do for a living. Questions about religion or place of birth are also to be avoided.

A rather more general danger is that of mechanical behaviour, with routine questions that never vary and contrived, stilted reactions. Some fear that this sort of chapter makes that type of robotic style more likely, but the aim of the chapter is to describe a range of ploys that readers will be able to use and practise within a framework of natural and spontaneous interaction. It is by understanding what is happening and becoming aware of the effect of different ploys that the interactor can bring vitality and realism to the interaction.

References

Beveridge, W. E., *Problem-Solving Interviews*, Allen & Unwin, London, 1968, pp. 57–58.

Higham, M., *The ABC of Interviewing*, Institute of Personnel Management, London, 1979, p. 133.

Malinowski, B., "The problem of meaning in primitive languages", in Ogden, C. K. and Richards, I. A. (eds), *The Meaning of Meaning*, Harcourt, Brace Jovanovich, New York, 1923.

Maude, B., *Communication at Work*, Business Books, London, 1977, p. 106.

Mayerson, E. W., *Shoptalk: Foundations of Managerial Communication*, Saunders, Philadelphia, 1979, p. 120.

Mayerson, E. W., *ibid.*, 1979(b), p. 117

Reik, T., *Listening with the Third Ear*, Grove Press, New York, 1948.

PART TWO

HANDLING TYPICAL SITUATIONS

Chapter 4

Structure and Types of Interaction

Procrustes was a robber of Ancient Greek legend who used the unusual device of a bed to torture his victims. The novelty was that Procrustes made sure that the bed fitted each occupant precisely. If he was too long, then hands or feet would be cut off; if he was too short he would be stretched. Either way the result was that the victim fitted the bed.

In this chapter we now run the risk of butchering the reality of inter-action by making it fit not one but two Procrustean beds, as the objective now is to provide two forms of classification: firstly types of encounter and then a structure for the encounters. The danger of this is that the classifications cannot be perfect and some encounters may be categorised in such a way as to obscure rather than clarify. There is also the risk of making readers think in a rigid rather than flexible way.

Despite the risks, the classification is generally useful and informa-tive, enabling people to see differences between encounters more clearly. It is important, for instance, to differentiate between an encounter where the basic job to be done is joint problem-solving and one where it is conflict resolution. They are different situations, involving different approaches, yet the way in which an encounter is handled often fails because of failure to make the distinction at the outset. If a manager faces a discussion with a group of shop stewards about a conflict of interests, it is the conflict which needs to be addressed. It is both pointless and damaging if he tries to ignore that very difficult task by talking blandly about "all being in the same boat" and needing "to pull together". Another example is the counselling interview. If problem-solving is required, the approach to the encounter is quite different from that of giving advice, however sound and well intentioned.

When people enter interactions it is with differing needs, perceptions and expectations. For the interaction to be effective the person leading in the exchange has to try and develop a degree of congruence between those opening differences.

> A lack of understanding regarding the communication rules of a particular relationship or situation may be the most serious of all possible breakdowns. Rules are the basis on which the communica-tion relationship must be constructed. If mutual understanding regarding the expectations of each participant can not be achieved, then it becomes impossible for interpersonal communication to occur. (Baskin and Aronoff, 1980)

Russell (1972) examined the degree of understanding between one hundred sales representatives and their immediate superiors in their communications together. His findings show the problems: in 60% of situations there was what Russell called *monolithic consensus* as both parties to the interaction agreed on the communications rules and their perceptions. In 20% of situations there was a *false consensus*, which meant that the participants disagreed, but believed they agreed. *Pluralistic ignorance* was the position which the parties agreed without knowing it and *dissensus* was where the parties disagreed and knew it. Both of these last two categories accounted for 10% of the responses.

The classification of encounter types goes some way to clarifying understanding about the varieties that exist and the expectations that are present. The classifications are not perfect, but will help the reader reflect upon his own personal performance in this most individual of activities. To this end the categorisation of encounter types and structures is useful not as a pattern to produce mechanical behaviour, but as a window through which to examine the activity.

4.1 Four Types of Interaction

Most of the interactions in organisational life can be put into one of the following four categories, although some span two or more.

4.1.1 Exposition

The expository interview is one in which the person in charge (referred to as the principal) has the main task of conveying some information or ideas to one or more other people. The principal knows "the answer" and his task is to transfer that as accurately as possible into the minds of the respondents. This is the simplest example of the communications process, with all the stress on encoding, sending the signal and collecting the feedback to test accuracy and modify later signals. The emphasis is completely on the principal making himself clear and getting the message across. There are many interactions that come under this general heading in working life. There is the one-word instruction "Fire!" and the many similar perfunctory orders: "Take this down to Mr Jones . . .", "Get another one from Stores . . .", "Offer them another 2½% if they settle this week . . .". As communications these are not too difficult, but in the same category of exposition are the more complex skills, reporting back, briefing, public-speaking and lecturing. In these situations the principal has to work harder at the exposition, with greater clarification and perhaps the need to convince the respondents against their better judge-

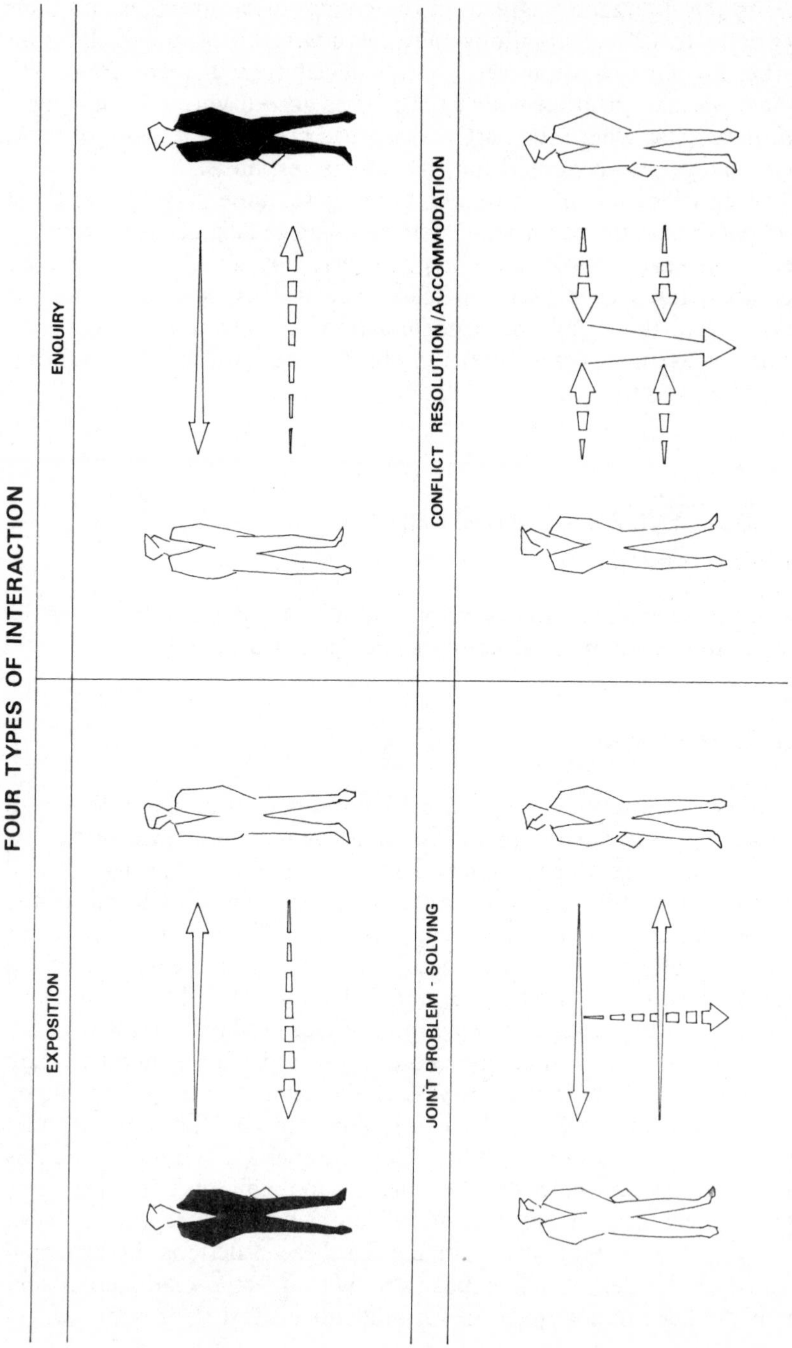

Fig. 4.1 The four categories of interaction: exposition, enquiry, problem-solving and conflict resolution.

ment. There is then a change of emphasis and a greater degree of skill required, but the task remains that of transferring what he knows across to the minds of the listeners. One of the most common difficulties here is when the principal tries to build his communication on the feedback, before there is any basis for the feedback, like the lecturer who went into the classroom of a further education college and began by saying to the class, "Well, I am in your hands, what would you like me to tell you?"

4.1.2 Enquiry

The opposite of exposition is enquiry, in which the principal has the main job of finding something out, obtaining rather than imparting information. He does not know "the answer" but has to discover it by gleaning it from the minds of his respondents. In the telecommunications analogy the principal is the receiver rather than the transmitter, but enquiry obviously involves more than simply tuning in to a signal that is being transmitted: the transmission has to be stimulated in the first place.

In working life the standard example of enquiry is the selection or employment interview. It is fashionable for people to talk of this encounter as being a two-way process, with the principal doing as much expounding as enquiry, but every candidate for interview sees it as enquiry with the information from the principal and his own opportunity to question the principal being either preliminaries to "the real thing" or appendages to put the candidate at his ease. Other examples are attitude surveys, market research interviewing, the analysis of training needs, preparing job descriptions and carrying out health checks. The effectiveness of the interaction will be a function of the accuracy with which the principal is able to build the picture in his own mind of what is in the mind of the other. Implicit in this is the lack of evaluation in the enquiry itself, as the principal concentrates on finding out what is in the mind of the respondent. Once he begins to evaluate what he is learning, then the accuracy of his enquiry will fade.

The chief skill in enquiry is questioning, to ensure that information flows mainly from the respondent to the principal. Some information will still flow in the opposite direction—from principal to respondent—to provide an acceptable base for the questions to be put and then to provide focus for the answers that are being offered. In this way the respondent is led to provide the requisite information. The market research interviewer, for instance, will have to provide some information at the beginning of his encounter to persuade the respondent even to stop and consider the questions. Once the respondent has agreed to participate the principal can move on to the questions, but the questions themselves will be worded to contain a steady flow of information as to what is needed. In this way the replies are accurate and informative.

4.1.3 Joint Problem-solving

The third category is quite different as "the answer" is not known to either party before the interaction begins. The task of the principal is not, therefore, to concentrate on accurate transfer of a picture from one mind to another, but rather to use an exchange of information to create a picture, which is helpful to both parties, but beyond the power of either to create single-handedly. It is a collaborative activity, requiring not only both participants to work together, but also a degree of mutual trust as each supports the other in a shared quest for understanding, which is a preliminary to making decisions and taking action. It is both more complex and more complete than interactions in the first two categories.

A useful example is career development interviewing, where the principal is a management development officer or personnel manager, thus having a responsibility to ensure that the respondent employee is making his expected contribution to organisational success – whatever that may be. The respondent is perhaps a management trainee, employed by the organisation for about a year and wanting to know whether he is making progress towards the glittering prizes at the top of the hierarchy, or whether he is failing in some way. They have to come together to talk about what is happening as each knows only a part of the story at the outset. They need to exchange information from their two different points of view as "the truth" of the matter lies in the composite picture of which separately they can only provide some components. Often the principal will have to begin by setting up a congruence of expectations between himself and the respondent, who will expect the omniscient principal to know "the answer" to the question, "How am I doing?" without the need for preliminary discussion. In those circumstances the preliminaries are regarded as cruel prevarication to "keeping me guessing" unless the principal works hard to explain a different mode of interaction and to get the respondent's acceptance of that mode.

There are other situations where the principal finds himself quite unexpectedly in joint problem-solving, where the respondent had signalled exposition or enquiry. The question over the telephone, "Can I call in and get you to explain this new pension scheme for a few minutes?" may turn out to be, "I can't make up my mind about whether or not to take early retirement".

4.1.4 Conflict Resolution/Accommodation

The final category is the most complex and time-consuming interaction of all, resolving – or finding an accommodation for – conflict. As with joint problem-solving it is an interaction where "the answer" is not known beforehand and the participants have to come together to fashion it. The fundamental difference between this and joint problem-solving is the low level of common interest, as the parties are seeking objectives which, to some extent, are against the interests of each other. The buyer of an aero-engine will seek the lowest possible price, while the seller will seek the highest possible price: they cannot both be completely satisfied. Neither, however, will seek his own ends at all costs. The buyer will want the seller to remain in business and continuing with research and development and the seller will not want to obtain one order but lose later opportunities because of overcharging. Although the opening positions of the two parties is seen as the optimum for each, they each have to take account of the opposing position in order to find a balance between their conflicting aims after testing the logic and strength of the opposition through open argument.

The position of the principal is less clear in conflict resolution/accommodation than in other encounters as the parties see themselves as being evenly matched in many instances, although the principal in some cases is a third person holding the ring. Arbitration and mediation are examples of this.

Sometimes these encounters are between individuals with third party involvement, as described by Walton (1969). Usually, however, they are collective activities with teams representing each side, as in negotiations between managers and shop stewards. Typically great emphasis is placed on following procedures and observing ritual requirements. There will probably be a high degree of anxiety and emotional stress present.

For the next part of this book a series of different interactions is examined in detail. There are two interactions in each of the four categories set out in this chapter, and the role of the principal is different in each case, requiring a varying range of behaviours, but the most important issue for the principal is to begin the interaction clear about his *role*:

Chapter	Interaction category	Type of interaction	Role of principal
5	Exposition	Training for skill	Tutor
6	Exposition	Making a speech	Exponent

continued overleaf

continued

Chapter	Interaction category	Type of interaction	Role of principal
7	Enquiry	The selection interview	Selector
8	Enquiry	The attitude survey	Investigator
9	Problem-solving	Counselling	Counsellor
10	Problem-solving	Discipline	Monitor
11	Conflict resolution	Negotiation	Negotiator
12	Conflict resolution	Arbitration	Arbitrator

4.2 Three Stages of Interaction

The main, loose framework for the next eight chapters is the three stages of preparation, encounter and follow-up, and few would argue that encounters do not have preparatory phases and subsequently need follow-up. That sequencing logic is, however, carried further by developing a sequence for interaction within each of the three stages. In most cases the text will argue that the sequence is necessary. This occurs, for instance, in chapter 11 where the activity of challenge and defiance is firmly placed before thrust and parry. In other instances the sequence is at least logical and occasionally it is arbitrary. As the performances we are discussing are those which depend for their success on individual ability, flair and judgement, the suggested sequencing should not be regarded as a tightly belted straitjacket allowing no movement whatsoever. On the other hand they should not be discarded or altered without thinking through the implications of such variation.

References

Baskin, O. W. and Aronoff, C. E., *Interpersonal Communication in Organizations*, Goodyear Publishing Co., Santa Monica, Calif., 1980, p. 35.

Russell, H. M., 1972, unpublished research dissertation quoted in Baskin and Aronoff, *op. cit.*

Walton, R. E., *Interpersonal Peacemaking: Confrontations and Third Party Consultation*, Addison-Wesley, Reading, Mass., 1969.

Chapter 5

Exposition I: Training for Skill

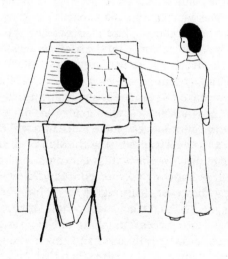

Teaching a person to *do* something requires a different approach from teaching someone to *understand* something. This broad distinction between training in skill and training in knowledge has been refined by the CRAMP taxonomy (ITRU, 1976), developed after a study of the work of the Belbins (Belbin and Belbin, 1972). This system divides all learning into five basic types. *Comprehension* is where the learning involves theoretical subject matter, knowing how, why and when certain things happen. Examples would be the laws of thermodynamics, the kings and queens of England or the currency structure of the EEC. *Reflex* learning is involved when skilled movements of perceptual capacities have to be acquired, involving practice as well as knowing what to do. Speed is usually important and the trainee needs constant repetition to develop the appropriate synchronisation and coordination. Obvious, but extreme, examples would be juggling and gymnastics; there are many working-life examples, of which typing may be the most common. *Attitude* development is concerned with enabling people to alter their attitudes and social skills. *Memory* training is obviously concerned with trainees developing the capacity to know how to handle a variety of given situations. Pharmacists learn by rote a series of maximum dosages, for example, and an office messenger will need to remember that all invoices go to Mr Brown and all cheques to Mr Smith. *Procedural* learning is similar to memory except that the drill to be followed does not have to be memorised, but located and understood.

In practice most forms of training involve more than one type of learning, so that the apprentice vehicle mechanic will need to understand how the car works as well as practising the skill of tuning an engine, and the driver needs to practise the skill of coordinating hands, feet and eyes in driving as well as knowing the procedure to follow if he breaks down. Broadly speaking, however, learning of the comprehension type is best approached by a method that teaches the whole subject as an entity rather than splitting it up into pieces and taking one at a time. Here the lecture or training manual are typically used and this is the subject of the next chapter. Attitude change is now often handled by group discussion to which there is reference in the final chapter of this book, but reflex learning is best handled by part methods, which break the task down into sections, each of which can be studied and practised separately before putting together a complete performance, just as a tennis player will practise the smash and then the forehand and the backhand and other individual strokes before playing a match in which all are used. Memory and procedural learning may take place either by whole or by part methods, although memorisation is usually best done by parts.

5.1 The Development of Learning Theory

Those working in education have studied the process of learning for many years. Much of the work has been associated with understanding child development, but the main contributions to modern learning theory are helpful to those teaching adults. Inevitably some of the most penetrating comments were made long ago. Plato avers that "knowledge obtained under compulsion obtains no hold on the mind" and thus reminds us of the need to win the commitment of the learner to that which is to be learned. The so-called Herbartian Formal Steps of preparation, presentation, association, generalisation and application are still widely used as a basis for lesson preparation, even though they were enunciated by J. F. Herbart at the University of Königsberg in the first decade of the nineteenth century. His notion of the orderly procedure is fundamental to the interaction structures which are set out in this book.

Probably the most significant principle in learning theory today is the Law of Effect, produced by E. L. Thorndike (1921), who began studying animals in 1896 and continued to research on humans forty years later. He formulated three laws:

(i) *The Law of Exercise.* The response to a situation becomes association with that situation, and the more it is used in a given situation, the more strongly it becomes associated with it. On the other hand, disuse of the response weakens the association.

(ii) *The Law of Effect.* Responses that are accompanied or closely followed by satisfaction are more likely to happen again when the situation recurs, while responses accompanied or closely followed by discomfort will be less likely to recur.

(iii) *The Law of Intensity.* The greater the satisfaction or discomfort the greater will be the strengthening or weakening between the situation and the response.

As Thorndike advanced his study of human beings he came to give much greater weight to reward than punishment (Thorndike, 1933). It is this type of reasoning which underpins the ideas of practice and what is nowadays called "reinforcement", whereby satisfactory performance is reinforced by rewards, such as praise and promotion.

Later research has questioned how basic to the process of learning reinforcement can actually be, for example:

Over the years . . . evidence has accumulated to indicate that learning is *not* fundamentally a matter of gradually strengthening of connections but rather an all-or-none event. Thus most modern theorists tend to favor the idea that the individual connection is acquired on a single occasion . . . The effects of repetition may be to recruit more and more single connections, but each one is either learned or not learned. (Gagne, 1975)

This is the line of reasoning that supports the holistic approach of comprehension-type learning. Understanding will come at the time when the penny eventually drops and a number of disconnected facts or ideas suddenly come together. To do this the learner develops a cognitive structure to preserve and organise what he is receiving so that the insight (the penny dropping) is made possible. Recently, researchers have been testing the hypothesis that there is a two stage process in human learning, with a short-term memory and a long-term memory. In your short-term memory you will hold the name of the person to whom you have just been introduced at a party, while in your long-term memory you will hold information like your own name. Much organisation of learning experiences is directed towards the processing of information so that it is translated from one memory bank to the other. One of the best examinations of this process is in Atkinson and Shiffrin (1968).

5.2 Reflex Learning of Motor Skills

The first step in learning a skill is for the trainee to understand the task and what he will need to do to produce a satisfactory performance. This provides the initial framework for, and explanation of, the actions that are to be developed later, although more information will be added to the framework as the training proceeds. The job of the tutor at this point is to decide how much understanding is needed to set up the training routine, especially if part methods are to be used for the later practice. An elementary skill is the pouring of molten lead into moulds to produce a "grid" that forms the basis of a lead–acid battery plate. To avoid waste and personal hazard a trainee will practise pouring sand instead of lead for a short spell. Unless he understands why he is pouring sand when he is training for a job in which he casts lead grids, he will not bring much application to his practice. The very long and detailed preliminary explanation, however, may be too much for trainees to follow before their "hands-on" experience.

The second step is to practise the performance and the task of the tutor is to decide how much division of the task into subroutines will aid learning. Typists begin their training by learning subroutines for each hand before combining them into routines for both hands together, but pianists spend very short periods of practice with one hand only. The reason for this seems to be that typists use their two hands in ways that are relatively independent of each other with the left always typing "a" and the right always typing "p", so that coordination of the hands is needed only to sequence the actions. In playing the piano there is a more complex integration of the actions performed by the two hands so that separate practice can impair rather than enhance later performance. A further aspect of learning to type is to practise short letter sequences that occur frequently, such as "and", "or", "the", "ing" and "ion". These can then be incorporated into the steadily increasing speed of the typist. A feature of this type of development is the extent to which the actions become automatic and reliable. The amateur typist will often transpose letters or hit the wrong key, writing "trasnpose" instead of "transpose" or "hte" instead of "the". The skilled typist will rarely do this because the effect of the repeated drills during training will have made the subroutines not only automatic but correct.

The third element in this type of training is feedback, so that the trainee can compare his own performance with the required standard and see the progress that he is making. The characteristics of good feedback are immediacy and accuracy. If the feedback comes immediately after the action the trainee has his best chance of associating error with the part of the performance that caused it, whereas delayed feedback will demonstrate what was wrong, but the memory of what happened will have faded. The boy learning to bowl straight at cricket will immediately be able to see how accurate his attempt was, and will be able to connect the degree of deviation with the position of his feet or angle of arm, or whatever caused the problem. The trainee photographer does not have that element of immediate feedback. The second characteristic of feedback is that it should be as accurate as possible in the information it provides on the result and the performance. The person coaching the trainee cricketer may say, "That's pretty good", or he may say, "That was the best ball so far, but it was still an inch or so too wide. Try to keep your arm higher as you bring it over". The second comment provides a general indication of making progress, it provides an assessment of the performance and specific comment that should improve the next attempt. Fitts and Posner (1967) elucidate this very helpfully.

5.3 A Structured Approach to Instruction

5.3.1 Preparation

(a) Objectives
There will be two sets of objectives, firstly organisational and secondly behavioural. Organisational objectives are a series that specify what is the contribution to the organisation that will be made by the trainee at the end of his training. It will be general but necessary. If a company trains its own typists, for instance, it might be that the organisational objectives will be to teach people to type and to transcribe from handwritten copy or dictating machine, but not to take short-hand. These are different from educational objectives, which focus on the trainee or student rather than on organisational needs, so that those instructing in secretarial colleges are much more likely to organise training round an appreciation of what will be useful in a number of occupational openings. For the tutor the potential conflict between organisational and educational objectives will have been resolved elsewhere as a matter of policy. In the training of apprentices, for instance, the industry training boards have considerable influence in ensuring that apprenticeships are broadly based and not a form of cheap labour providing narrow and restricted training, but some employers provide training that goes far beyond the basic requirements by arranging adventure training, camps, expeditions and other projects with a vague character-building objective. The tutor will need to work out organisational objectives which may or may not include broader educational features.

Behavioural objectives are specifically what the trainee should be able to do when the training, or training phase, is complete. Organisational objectives for typist trainees may be simply to ensure a constant supply of people able to type accurately and at reasonable speed. In behavioural terms that would be more specific by setting standards for numbers of words to be typed to a predetermined level of accuracy per minute. Cicero (1973) provides a typical example about servicing photocopying equipment:

> Given a tool kit and a service manual, the technical representative will be able to adjust the registration (black line along paper edges) on a Xerox 2400 duplicator within 20 minutes according to the specification stated in the manual.

(b) Learning methods
Next the tutor will decide what learning methods are to be used. We have

already seen that the main elements of skill training are understanding, practice and feedback, so the tutor will decide how much initial explanation is needed, and how many other explanations at different stages of the training, together with the form that is appropriate. Words alone may be enough, but audio-visual illustration and demonstration will probably be needed as well.

The two questions about practice are to decide on the subroutines and any necessary simulation, like the man pouring sand instead of lead. Most feedback is by the tutor talking to the trainee, but it may be necessary to devise ways of providing greater accuracy or speed to the feedback by methods like television recording or photography. The most common method for teaching motor skills is the *progressive part* method that had its most comprehensive explanation by Douglas Seymour (1966). The task to be undertaken by the trainee is broken down into a series of subroutines. The trainee then practises routine 1, routine 2 and then 1 + 2. The next step is to practise routine 3, 2 + 3 and 1 + 2 + 3, so that competence is built up progressively by practising a subroutine and then attaching it to the full task, which is constantly being practised with an increasing number of the different components included. The components are only practised separately for short periods before being assimilated so that there is no risk of fragmentary performance.

This only works if the job can be subdivided into components. Where this is not possible, *simplification* offers an alternative. In this method the task to be performed is kept as a whole, but reduced to its simplest form. Skilled performance is then reached by gradually increasing the complexity of the exercises. An example is the new art of candle-making. Fancy candles are made by cutting strips down the side of multi-coloured candle blocks and fashioning the strips into elaborate confections. The candle-maker is trained by starting to make candles with little elaboration and gradually increasing the flights of fancy.

Although this chapter is concerned mainly with motor skill training, there are some specialised methods of memory training which can be listed here, as well as ways of training for perceptual skill. Both types of ability appear to be increasing in importance in organisational life.

The most familiar way of memorising is the *mnemonic* or *jingle*, wherein a simple formula provides the clue to a more comprehensive set of data. ASH is easier to remember than Action on Smoking and Health, NIBMAR soon became the code for No Independence Before Majority Rule and all those who were employed at the time of the 1971 Industrial Relations Act will remember the sacred words TINA LEA that were intoned or inscribed to demonstrate that This Is Not A Legally Enforceable Agreement. If the initial letters are not easily memorable, the mnemonic is replaced by the jingle. The denseness of ROYGBIV has led generations of school children to remember that Richard Of York Gave Battle In Vain as a way of recalling the spectrum, and the indifference of science teachers to historical accuracy is shown by the fact that there is another school of thought using the jingle, Richard Of York Gained Battles In Vain. For some tasks the use of *rules* reduces the volume of material to be memorised. There are many fault-finding rules, for instance, where the repairer is taught to use a systematic series of rules. The stranded motorist who telephones the vehicle rescue service for assistance will probably be asked a first question, "Have you run out of petrol?" The answer "Yes" identifies the fault, while "No" leads to the second question, "Is there any spark?" so that the patrolman who comes to help already has some areas of fault eliminated. *Deduction* is a method that puts information into categories so that if something does not fit into one category the trainee then uses deduction to conclude that it must belong in another. At the beginning of this chapter was the example of the office messenger remembering that invoices go to Mr Brown and cheques to Mr Smith. If there was also a Mr Robinson, who received all sales enquiries, complaints, unsolicited sales promotion material, post-cards, tax returns, questionnaires, applications for employment and so on, the messenger would obviously not need to remember what *did* go to Mr Robinson, but what did not: invoices to Mr Brown, cheques to Mr Smith and everything else to Mr Robinson. Some interesting examples of using deduction in training are to be found in Belbin and Downs (1966). For memorisation of information the *cumulative part* is slightly, but significantly, different from the progressive part method already described in that the trainee constantly practises the whole task, with each practice session adding an extra component. This is distinct from progressive part in which components are practised separately before being built into the whole. This can be especially useful if the more difficult material is covered first, as it will then get much more rehearsal than that coming later.

Turning now to the development of perceptual skills, one method is known as *discrimination*, whereby the trainee learns to distinguish between items that appear similar to the untrained eye or ear, nose or fingertip. In a rough-and-ready way it is the procedure followed by the birdwatcher or the connoisseur of wine. First the trainee compares two items which are clearly dissimilar and identifies, or has described to him, the points of difference. Then other pairs are produced for him to compare, with the differences gradually becoming less obvious. Discrimination can be aided by *cueing*, which helps the trainee to identify particular features in the early attempts at discrimination by giving them the assistance of arrows or coloured sections. Some people spend a part of their time learning to type with the keys coloured according to whether they should be struck with the left or right hand, or even according to the particular finger which is appropriate. Gradually the cues are phased out as the trainee acquires the competence to identify without cues. *Magnification* is a method of developing the capacity to distinguish small faults in a process or even small components in machinery. As the name implies the material is increased in size at the beginning of training and then reduced back to normal as competence is acquired. Inspectors of tufted carpet start their training by being shown samples of poor tufting that have been contrived using much larger material than normal. Later they examine normal material under a magnifying glass and eventually they are able to examine the normal product. A helpful discussion of magnification method can be found in Holding (1965).

(c) Training programme

The various training methods that are to be used are orchestrated into a training or instructional programme. This sets out not only what the tutor is going to do, as his plan of action, but also the progress the trainee is expected to make. Of critical importance here is *pacing*; how much material the trainee has to take in before practice begins, how long he has to practise before he is able to proceed to a new part, and how frequently his progress is checked by the tutor. Each trainee will have his own rate at which he can proceed and the amount of initial explanation and demonstration he needs before practice can start. For this reason training programmes have to be flexible so as to accommodate the varying capacities that learners bring to the training.

A useful feature of the training programme is scope for the trainee to be involved in both determining his rate of progress and some self-discovery, so that he is not spoon fed. At the outset he is so conscious of his dependency that all measures are useful if they will build up his confidence, independence and autonomy.

(d) Selection of trainees

The last feature of preparation is selecting those to be trained. The emphasis will be on basic suitability of individuals for the course that is planned, so that training for a skill requiring deft manipulation will be preceded by selection that establishes either previous success in work involving similar dexterity or potential for such accomplishment that may be determined by aptitude tests. Another consideration is the compatability of trainees who are going to be working together. If a tutor has a number of occasions on which training is to be provided, he may try to group trainees together with rough similarities of age, experience or aptitude that will make them reasonably homogenous in the rate at which they are likely to advance.

5.3.2 Encounter

(a) Meeting

When tutor and trainee meet for the first time there is a mutual appraisal. The process is as described under *rapport* in chapter 3, but the "getting-to-know-you" exchanges are more important than most of the encounters described in this book, as the two people have to work together and the trainee will be acutely aware of his own ignorance and uncertainty in an unfamiliar situation. He is absolutely dependent upon the tutor, who has the capacity to bring the trainee to understanding, competence at the task, acceptance in the social system of the organisation and self-confidence resulting from achievement. The tutor needs to resist the temptation to make the most of the brief opportunity to play God. The trainee needs to feel confidence in the instructor as someone skilled in the task that is to be learned and enthusiastic about teaching it to others. He will also be looking for reassurance about his own chances of success by seeking information about previous trainees. All of us seek to manipulate and master our environment and the first-day trainee will instinctively be looking for ways in which to establish some prospect of such mastery.

(b) Explaining procedure

The explanation of procedure will follow as soon as the meeting phase has lasted long enough. Here is the first feature of pacing that was mentioned as part of preparation. There has to be enough time for meeting to do its work, but long, drawn-out introductions can lead to impatient chafing and wanting to get started.

The procedure is the programme, with the associated details of timing, rate of progress, training methods and the general overview of what is to happen. The most important point to the trainee is obviously the end. When does he "graduate"? What happens then? Can it be quicker? Do many people fail? What happens to them? The tutor is, of course, more interested in the beginning of the programme rather than the end, but it is only with a clear grasp of the end that the trainee can concentrate later on the beginning. He has to set his sights and get the goal clear in order to find the commitment to learning. With long-running training programmes where an array of skills has to be mastered, the point of graduation may be too distant to provide an effective goal so

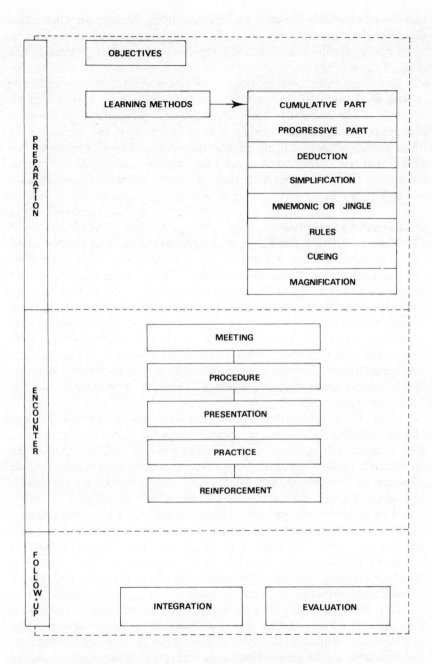

Fig. 5.1 A structured approach to instruction.

that the tutor establishes intermediate goals: "By Friday you will be able to . . .".

This phase will usually benefit from some illustration; a timetable, a chart of the average learning curve, samples of work by previous trainees all make more tangible the prospect of success and more complete the picture of the operating framework that the trainee is putting into his mind. It is also helpful to avoid the explanation becoming mechanical, like the tourist guide at Windsor Castle. If the tutor has explained the procedure so often that it has become automatic, it is not the apotheosis of skill that was described earlier. It is a time for as much interchange as possible, with questions, reiteration, further explanation, clarification and confirmation.

(c) Presenting the task

The task that the trainee has to perform first is demonstrated and explained to him. The purpose is not to display the tutor's advanced skills, but to provide a basis for the trainee's first, tentative (and possibly incorrect) attempts. The demonstration is thus done without any flourishes or extras, and as slowly as possible, because the tutor is using his skill to convince the trainee that he *can* do the job. Accompanying the demonstration the explanation gives reasons why the different actions are being used and describing what is being done so that the trainee can watch analytically. His attention is drawn to a feature of the subroutine that he might overlook, the sequence of actions is recounted and key points are mentioned.

One of G. K. Chesterton's aphorisms was, "If a thing is worth doing, it is worth doing badly", and this would be a good motto for the trainee's first attempts. The tutor must enable him quickly to do the job badly: the car must at least start instead of stall; the typewriter must reproduce "the quick brown fox jumped over the lazy dog", even if the letters are untidy. The task must be presented to the trainee in its simplest possible form, with a straightforward, unfussy, accurate demonstration accompanied by an explanation which emphasises correct sequence, reasons why, features that might be overlooked in the demonstration and the key points that lead to success. Where possible, the tutor should not mention what *not* to do. Incorrect aspects of performance can be dealt with later, at this stage the direction should be on what to do.

The presentation is followed, and perhaps interrupted, by questions from the trainee on what he did not follow or cannot remember. The success of this will depend on the skill of the tutor in going through the opening stages of the encounter. Many trainees are reluctant to question because they feel that the question reveals their ignorance and they fear that ignorance will be judged as stupidity. The experienced tutor can stimulate the questioning and confirming by the trainee through putting questions to them. This is effective only when done well, as there is the obvious risk of inhibiting people by confronting them with their lack of understanding. The most unfortunate type of questions are those which cross-examine:

"Now, tell me the three main functions of this apparatus".
"Can anyone remember which switch we press first?"

Little better are the vague requests for assent:

"Do you understand?"
"Am I making myself clear?"
"Is that all right, everybody?"

These are like the leading questions we looked at in chapter 3. They will be some use as there will be nods and grunts from the trainees to provide response, but it is most unlikely that people will do more than offer the easy, regular "yes". The job of the tutor is to help the trainee build the picture in his own mind without the feeling that he is being tested. This will only come with good rapport, but if he has managed interchange in explaining procedure, then it may carry over into the presentation.

(d) Practice
After the presentation the trainee has his first attempt at the subroutine. He expects to do badly, and needs confidence from the tutor, who has to avoid two common pitfalls: too much or too little intervention.

If the tutor intervenes too much the trainee is not "feeling his feet" and acquiring the confidence that comes from sensing the strength and purpose of his own first faltering steps. Too little intervention means that the trainee learns about his lack of competence, which is reinforced by a performance which falls short of what presentation had suggested as being possible. This shows the importance again of presentation, which has to be pitched at the level that will make initial performance feasible, without building up expectations that cannot be realised.

Among the considerations for tutors are the varying potential of individual trainees and the ritual elements of training. Some trainees will be able to make initial progress much more rapidly than others, so that pegging all to the same rate of advance will inhibit both. The ritual features depend on the acknowledgement by the trainee of the absolute, albeit temporary, superiority of the tutor. It has already been pointed out that there is a reluctance to question during presentation; there are also intermittent displays of deference to the tutor. This enables trainees to perform badly during practice without losing face. However, deference to a superior figure is normally offered on the assumption that the acolyte is being helped to make his own way to the advanced state of grace that the superior enjoys. If early practice of a taught skill produces an abject performance by the trainee, then he is moving further away from the desired state of grace and he either loses confidence or he resents the instructor for highlighting the trainee's inadequacy.

Learning theory tells us the importance of the law of effect, which practice makes possible, but it also tells us that there is likely to be a point at which the trainee makes a sudden leap forward—the point at which the penny drops and there is a shared excitement. In the words of Professor Higgins about Eliza: "I think she's got it. By Jove, she's got it". Practice leads up to the point where the learning spurts forward and it then provides the reinforcement of that learning by continued rehearsal and confirmation.

(e) Reinforcement

The most effective reinforcement for the trainee is when he sees for himself that he can perform, like the child who finds that he can at last remain erect and mobile on a bicycle. Seldom can the trainee rely on his own interpretation of success: he will need his work constantly assessed by the tutor. Many of the text books on teaching and learning emphasise the value of praise, a little of which apparently goes a long way, for example:

> When they are learning people need to know where they stand, they need to know how they are progressing. The knowledge of their progress spurs them on to greater achievements. In this respect praise is always far more helpful than criticism. (Winfield, 1979)

The reservation about this is the substantive nature of the praise that is provided. It is of little value if it is mechanical, repetitive and non-discriminating. With training in routine tasks, tutors frequently fall into this trap, with stereotyped responses. It is similar to the problems mentioned in chapter 3 about establishing rapport.

Effective reinforcement is that in which the trainee sees for himself and can understand both the result and the actions or behaviour which produced the result, so the tutor needs to identify the particular ways in which progress is being made and explain their merit, as well as explaining what caused the progress to happen. When the trainee is approaching full competence, with the associated self-confidence, then he is able to cope with more direct criticism.

5.3.3 Follow-up

(a) Integration
The first follow-up step to a training episode is when the trainee integrates his new learning with his existing store of knowledge, understanding and skill so as to extend his overall performance potential. These are the Herbartian steps of Association and Generalisation. This may be done by the trainee alone, but more probably with the tutor. The new facet of skill is placed in a number of different contexts so that the learned subroutine makes possible a whole range of new possibilities. Once the apprentice has learned to plane the edge of a piece of wood smooth, he needs to appreciate how that ability, of itself valueless, can be made valuable by combining it with other subroutines. The sequence of explanation, demonstration and practice begins once more.

(b) Evaluation
Evaluating the effectiveness of the training episode will increase the tutor's store of knowledge for dealing with future trainees. Simple methods are the most reliable, like records of the time taken to reach the different levels of effectiveness.

(c) Checking progress and coaching
It is not often possible for the tutor to carry out the helpful job of checking on the progress of the trainee after training is complete. It is common for the trainee to pass beyond the tutor's ken and perform as an experienced worker under a different regime, where someone else – a charge-hand or supervisor – takes over the responsibility for performance standards. In some circumstances it is, however, possible for the tutor to keep in touch with ex-trainees in a coaching capacity. He can then spot aspects of slack practice that are beginning to develop or help with overcoming a temporary problem. This is not an easy role, as the line manager may be uneasy about the effect of the intervention and the trainee may not welcome his inexperience being emphasised among his new colleagues. Coaching remains, nevertheless, a helpful follow-up activity for the tutor when it is politically feasible.

(d) Changing methods
The tutor will regularly consider changes and improvements to his training methods. Although on-going, such change prospects come into clearest focus when a training programme has been completed.

References

Atkinson, R. C. and Shiffrin, R. M., "Human memory: a proposed system and its control processes", in Spence, K. and Spence, J., *The Psychology of Learning and of Motivation: Advances in Research & Theory*, Academic Press, New York, 1968.

Belbin, E. and Belbin, R. M., *Problems in Adult Retraining*, Heinemann, London, 1972.

Belbin, E. and Downs, S. "Teaching and paired associates", *Journal of Occupational Psychology*, **40**, 67–74, 1966.

Cicero, J. P., "Behavioural objectives for technical training systems", *Training and Development Journal*, **28**, 15, 1973.

Fitts, P. M. and Posner, M. J., *Human Performance*, Brooks Cole, Belmont, California, 1967, pp. 27–33.

Gagne, R. M., *Essentials of Learning for Instruction*, Holt Rinehart & Winton, New York, 1975, p. 14.

Holding, D. H., *Principles of Training: Research in Applied Learning*, Pergamon, Oxford, 1965.

ITRU (Industrial Training Research Unit), *Choose an Effective Style: a Self-Instructional Approach to the Teaching of Skills*, ITRU Publications, Cambridge, 1976.

Seymour, W. D., *Industrial Skills*, Pitman, London, 1966.

Thorndike, E. L., *Educational Psychology, Vol. II: The Psychology of Learning*, Teachers' College, Columbia University, New York, 1921.

Thorndike, E. L., *An Experimental Study of Rewards*, Teachers' College, Columbia University, New York, 1933.

Winfield, I., *Learning to Teach Practical Skills*, Kogan Page, London, 1979, p. 81.

Chapter 6

Exposition II:
Making a Speech

Demosthenes devoted his life to stirring up his fellow Athenians to resist the imperial dreams of Philip of Macedon. He did this through a series of speeches known as "Philippics" that were so successful that the Athenians marched against Philip—even though they were then beaten! Speaking to an audience has been one of the ways in which men have achieved power and influence over others, partly because of the importance of their message and partly because of the emotional power of their delivery of that message. It has been an assertion of leadership and symbolic of authority. In the careers of charismatic leaders significant stages are often highlighted by speeches: Paul of Tarsus on the Areopagus in Athens, Henry V rallying his troops before Agincourt, Lincoln at Gettysburg and Churchill during the Battle of Britain are all examples. The most extreme instance of such influence was probably Adolf Hitler:

> Speech was an essential medium of his power, not only over his audiences but over his own temperament. Hitler talked incessantly, often using words less to communicate his thoughts than to release the hidden spring of his own and others' emotions, whipping himself and his audience into anger or exaltation by the sound of his voice. (Bullock, 1969)

There is little scope for this type of oratory in organisational life, though there are frequent attempts by individual managers and trade union officials to incorporate aspects of propaganda into addresses they make to groups of employees in an attempt to change the attitudes and behaviour of members of the audience.

More common in working life are addresses intended to increase the knowledge and understanding of audience members, as on a training course, a sales presentation, a report to employees on company progress and so on. The most accurate term for this type of address is *the lecture*, but this still carries strong overtones of authority being imposed. In everyday conversation a comment like, "I had quite a lecture from her" is used to describe a rebuke or "putting-down" by an organisational superior.

This chapter will deal with exposition intended to increase knowledge and understanding, even though there are occasional references to persuasion.

As was shown in the telecommunication analogy, for knowledge and understanding to be augmented the emphasis should be on the way in which the exponent enables the members of the audience to understand rather than satisfying himself that he has included all the relevant information to his own satisfaction. Success lies in getting the message received and understood: not in transmitting it. Furthermore there may be many different receivers, all of whom have to be kept switched on and tuned in by the exponent. In selection, counselling, market research and discipline there is only one receiver; in training there will seldom be more than five or six and arbitration and negotiation also involve only small groups. Speaking to an audience will usually involve dozens or hundreds of receivers. Another important difference between this inter-action and others is the length of transmission. There is not the scope for two-way traffic that there is in the other situations, yet the multitude of receivers will all be operating at varying levels of efficiency. Some will be working efficiently while others are switched to another channel. Some will be producing one decoding of the message while others are producing another. It would be unduly optimistic to say that the exponent should get all the receivers working on the same wavelength in the same way.

This can be illustrated by examples from entertainment. As the performance at a pop concert becomes more frenzied and libidinous nearly all members of the audience will combine in a united response, with postural echoes, hands high above heads, glazed expressions and general ecstasy. Some, however, will react quite differently, sitting silent or inattentive. Even if a comedian is getting a steadily rising level of laughter from his audience with every succeeding joke, he will never make all the audience laugh.

The exponent in the lecture room or at the shareholders' meeting or the sales conference will never get everyone on his side, but he is putting on a performance, needing to win over as many members of the audience as possible. As with other performances there is scope for preparation, rehearsal and careful manipulation of the physical environment to achieve the maximum effect. This is why there is more emphasis on preparation in this chapter than in any of the others.

6.1 A Structured Approach to Exposition

6.1.1 Preparation

(a) The status of the exponent

Is the exponent the right person to deliver *this* message to *this* audience? The audience will turn up their receivers if the exponent has prestige; if he has not, they will turn off or not even tune in. The main determinant of appropriateness to deliver a message is the credence the audience gives to the exponent's standing and expertise. If they see him as having some information that will be of use to them, then they will accord him the necessary status and attend to what he says. If the ensuing exposition disappoints them they will not only become inattentive, they are likely to signal their disillusion with demoralising clarity. Audiences show little compunction about humiliating exponents, because the relationship is one in which the exponent is assuming authority with all its ritual trappings, such as standing while the audience sits, occupying special, distant space and anticipating their silence while he speaks. The attitude of the exponent to the members of the audience will also influence their attentiveness. He will be more acceptable if he seems well disposed to them and trying to tune in to them, than if he appears aloof, hostile or resentful so that they are expected to make the effort to tune in to him.

Another aspect of status is hierarchical. Senior members of organisations are expected to speak on important matters. When the level of the message is not consonant with the level of the exponent then there will be mistrust. To cite two actual examples. If the general manager calls a meeting of all the shop stewards simply to announce that the toilet doors are to be painted white the members of the audience will disperse asking each other what he really meant. If a lowly-placed charge-hand announces that the factory is to close then the audience will not believe him and demand corroboration, although, interestingly enough, that message will be taken more seriously. The small exception to this is the way in which those with power can invest it in their close aides, like the Buckingham Palace spokesman. In informal situations, at least, private secretaries and personal assistants to managing directors speak with considerable authority.

(b) The room

If the exponent can influence the arrangements of the room in which he has to speak, he has the opportunity to improve the quality of his eventual performance. Referring to the manipulation of space (see p. 21) the distance between the exponent and the audience needs clearly to be that of the public zone. The exponent will use eye contact as a means of control with the audience and this is made more difficult if anyone is too close. Also the seating is best arranged so that there are approximately the right number of seats. Too many will tend to scatter the members of the audience making it harder for the exponent to get them to behave like an audience rather than a scattering of individuals.

The position from which to speak is obviously dictated by the arrangements for the audience, but some of the typical problems are a lack of anywhere to put notes, a distracting background behind the speaker, or some problem with visual aids. Visual aids are referred to shortly, but the problem of the distracting background is not always appreciated. The audience need to look at the exponent so as to concentrate their minds on what he is saying. If he directs their attention to a screen or a blackboard he is directing their attention to something that should embellish what he is saying. Other visual images will be a distraction. Examples are murals or stained glass windows. Think of the blackboard or the chart on the wall. Exponents who scorn the blackboard because they have a sheaf of acetate sheets to show on the overhead projector often overlook the fact that members of the audience will tend to read what is on the blackboard, even though it was written by someone else the day before. One large company, for example, has a lecture room in its training centre that is used for management training sessions. On the wall to one side of the exponent's position is a wall chart of the periodic table of chemical elements. A training officer tells how he notices that all members of an audience spend some time examining the chart, whether they be chemists making sure they can remember the sequence or non-chemists trying to understand it. Strangely he does not turn the chart round so that people are not distracted from what he is saying. Alternatively some backgrounds may enhance a message in a subliminal way, like the stained glass window behind the head of the preacher.

(c) The material

What is to be said or, more accurately, what should members of the audience go away having understood and remembered? This is the basis of preparing for the exposition and organising what has to be said. The starting point is a *plan* with the three elements of introduction, substance and conclusion. In the introduction the exponent sets up rapport with the audience. Apart from his confidence and manner in winning their attention he will include here an answer to the unspoken question – is it going to be worth our while listening to this chap? He will set up the talk which is to come by explaining what he is going to say or what the members of the audience will know or be able to do at the end of it. It is also helpful to sketch out the framework of what is to come, so that people can follow it more readily. If he says there are going to be five points, they will listen for five to make sure that they have not missed one. In the substance is the message that is to be conveyed, the development of the argument and the build-up of what it is that the audience should go away having understood and remembered. The conclusion is where the main points of the substance are reiterated and confirmed in a brief, integrated summary.

In the substance there will be a number of key thoughts or *ideas*.

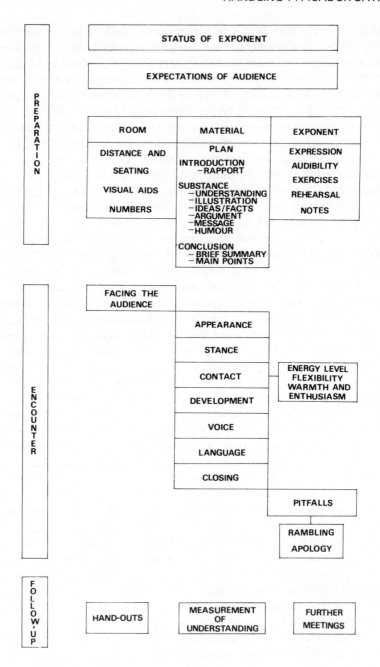

Fig. 6.1 A structured approach to exposition.

This is what the exponent will be trying to plant in the minds of the audience: not facts, which are inert, but the ideas which facts may well illustrate and clarify. The idea that unemployment is dangerously high is only illustrated by the fact that it is at a particular figure in a particular month. The ideas in an exposition can be helpfully linked together by a device that will help audience members to remember them all and to grasp their interdependence. One method is to enshrine the ideas in a story. If the story is recalled the thoughts are recalled with it, as they are integral to the structure. The classic examples of this are the New Testament parables, but every play, novel or film uses the same method. Another method is to use key words to identify the points that are being made, especially if they have an alliterative or mnemonic feature, like "Planning Progress and Prosperity". In a lecture it is common to provide a framework for ideas by using a drawing or system model to show the interconnection of points. The figures illustrating chapters 5–12 in this book are of that type.

Facts keep together the framework of ideas that the exponent has assembled by giving cogency to those ideas. They clarify and give dimension to what is being said. The danger is to use too many, so that the audience are overwhelmed by facts and figures which come to bemuse them.

Humour is the most dangerous of all aids to the exponent. If he tells a funny story and the audience laugh it will be most encouraging for him and relieve any tension that may be present – in him or in the audience – but how tempting to try again and end up "playing for laughs". Laughter is a most seductive human reaction, but too many laughs are even more dangerous than too many facts. What will the audience remember – the joke, or what the joke was to illustrate? Attempted humour is also dangerous for the ineffective comedian. If you tell what you think is a funny story and no-one laughs, you have made a fool of yourself (at least in your own eyes) and risk floundering. Very few people speak effectively without *notes*, despite the tendency to marvel at those who can manage it. Relying solely on memory there is the risk of missing something out, getting a fact wrong or drying up completely. Notes provide a discipline and restrain the tendency to ramble. How irritating it is for members of an audience to maintain attention when the speaker "pauses for a moment to mention in passing" something that inteferes with their attempt to keep hold on their own mental picture of the address.

There are basically two kinds of notes: headlines or a script. Headlines are probably the most common method, with main points underlined and facts listed beneath. Sometimes there will also be a marginal note about an anecdote or other type of illustration that would be relevant at different points. Figure 6.2 is an example taken from the notes of a sales manager addressing a sales conference.

The alternative of the script enables the exponent to try out his exact wording, phrases and pauses to achieve what he believes will be the greatest effect. The script will benefit from some marking or arrangement that will assist the exponent to find his place again as his eyes constantly flick from the page to the audience and back again. This can be underlining or painting over certain words and phrases with transparent, luminous ink. Another method of organising a script for an exposition is to use a form of blank verse. The best-known user of this method was Winston Churchill, but Peter Marshall, the Scottish-born Chaplain of the United States at the end of the Second World War, used a similar method for sermon notes. Figure 6.3 shows how this method not only helps the exponent find his place, but also gives cues for pauses and emphasis.

Points	Facts				Quotes etc.
1. Our market share has declined over the last year.	*Period*	*Us*	*Co.A*	*Others*	(a) Comment by JB at advertising agency.
	J–M	27%	22%	51%	
	A–J	24%	26%	50%	
	J–S	25%	25%	50%	(b) Story from
	O–D	22%	27%	51%	customer Z.
2. Not due to production difficulties.	(a) No stoppages in period.				Questions from
	(b) Production has *risen* 3%.				works convener at
	(c) Customer complaints on quality *down*.				production committee.

Fig. 6.2   Notes: headlines.

It is not easy to live out your life day after day
    and week after week
  and year after year in a subordinate position,
while somebody else gets the notice
              the publicity
              the attention
              the credit
              the praise
              the spotlight
        and perhaps the reward   (Marshall, 1954, p. 51)

Fig. 6.3   Notes: script.

(d) The exponent

The final feature of preparation is of the exponent himself, who has to bring the notes to life. *Rehearsal* can help eliminate potential difficulties but it depends on a third party to listen and comment on what is being said. Only in this way will there be an indication of what is heard and understood, as well as what is being said. So the first rehearsal check is on the clarity of expression. The second is on audibility. Occasional speakers find it difficult to speak loud enough to be heard at the same time as speaking naturally. Also there is a strange tendency to drop the voice at the end of sentences, losing the last few words.

Few people avoid *stage fright*. To some extent this is useful as it keys up the exponent to produce a vivid performance. Too much stage fright, however, can destroy it. Confidence is an essential feature in getting the audience to listen. Diffidence and nervousness may be engaging qualities in athletes who have just broken a world record or in bridegrooms at wedding receptions, but for most exponents it is an impediment. It can be reduced by deliberate relaxation, moving consciously a little more slowly than usual and concentrating on the deliberate relaxation of different muscles. Much can be achieved by breathing exercises, as advocated by Winifred Marks:

> It is relaxing simply to take several long, deep breaths, filling the base of the lungs and activating the diaphragm. More sophisticated techniques have been advocated, such as holding the nose between thumb and middle finger, with the index finger on the bridge and pressing the nostrils in turn to enforce breathing through each one alternately. (Marks, 1980, p. 51)

A less complicated method is to breathe in to a steady count of three and out to an equally steady count of nine; in to four and out to twelve; in to five and out to fifteen and so on. Marks also makes the interesting suggestion that the exponent should smile as much as possible before starting, as this will remove traces of an anxious frown and relax facial muscles before confronting the audience.

6.1.2 Encounter

Now begins the experience that some people find more frightening than any other: facing the audience. Sometimes the result can be exhilarating; all too frequently it is humiliating. The ritual is of one person asserting authority over others and the exponent cannot avoid the role in which he is cast. Disclaimers, apologies and appeals to the better nature of the audience are of no use as the only reason for the event in the first place is because in some way he *is* an authority and that is the expectation of the audience to which he has to rise. The audience that is satisfied will "applaud" and flatter the exponent in a dozen ways: the dissatisfied audience is merciless in its deprecation.

(a) Rapport

The method of rapport is basically as described on p.43 but its importance is greater and its development has more features. *Appearance* is particularly important, not in the sense of best suits or polished shoes, but what the appearance of the exponent says to the audience. The way in which we present ourselves to others says something of our attitude towards them – we have taken trouble to get ready, or we have not. This may be regarded as the trivia of manners, but virtually everyone works on their appearance to create an effect. An audience will scrutinise the exponent's appearance closely as they are trapped by him, with very little else to look at. Does he *look* prepared and organised? Does he *look* as if he cares what they think? Appearance can also distract. How much further is that zip going to slide in the next twenty minutes? I wonder where she got those earrings? I'm sure he's got odd socks on. That bracelet must have cost a fortune.

Stance is an expression of authority: you stand, they have to sit. This is an aspect of posture that was discussed on p. 30. It is not always essential to stand as the organisation of the room will probably give you enough special space to maintain your authority while sitting, but you deny yourself the opportunity for building up initial confidence slightly if you do not take this opportunity. The exponent's confident manner is an important feature in making the audience believe that it is all going to be worthwhile. It is not enough, but it is a noteworthy aspect of the opening.

The exponent will also demonstrate and foster his *contact* with the audience and involvement with them. One way to do this is to explain the structure of the exposition, the reasons for it, why the exponent is the person doing it, what the outcome could be for members of the audience. He needs to avoid the risk of creating false hopes, as it is pointless to generate a positive response at the beginning which is let down by the remainder of the performance so that the audience leaves disgruntled. The best method of contact is to look at the audience. This is difficult for inexperienced exponents, who regard the audience as a Hydra-headed monster and dare not look it in the eye, preferring to gaze intently either at their notes, a spot on the floor six inches in front of their feet or the top right hand corner of the ceiling. Such faint hearts should remember another figure from Greek mythology – the Gorgon, one glance from whom turned the observer to stone. The roles of speaker and listener are so clearly dominant and submissive respectively that the member of the audience who sees the exponent looking at him will appear interested, stop yawning, sit up straight, stop talking, defer the crossword till later or whatever other behaviour is consistent with being observed by an authority figure.

Mayerson suggests that there are three significant non-verbal cues that the exponent gives to affect audience response. The first is *energy level*:

> If he looks as if he needs a lectern to prop him up, he conveys a low energy level. If he seems bursting with vigor, he conveys a high energy level. The freedom with which he turns his head, smiles and moves his hands, the control of the breath as he sends forth his words, his speech volume, his articulation, and his spacing and pausing all contribute to an image of energy level. (Mayerson, 1979, p. 183)

Secondly is *flexibility* of movement and thirdly comes the exponent's *warmth and enthusiasm*:

> Enthusiasm is contagious. If a speaker wants to convince, he has to believe in the issue himself. His belief helps to get the message across. There is a difference between 'We have to do something about wasted materials' said as the speaker picks lint off his trousers, scans the horizon, stifles a yawn, or scratches his head, and 'We have to do something about wasted materials' said with inflection, pausing, direct eye contact and an erect posture. (Mayerson, 1979, p. 184)

(b) Development

After the audience has been won over – and even if it hasn't! – the exponent moves to develop his argument. The form of development is predetermined by the preparation that has been made: the number of ideas, the relevant facts, the illustrations and so on. It is now that the value of that preparation is felt. The exponent should not, however, fall into the trap of thinking that his opening funny story, with eye contact and a list of points to be covered is all the "performance" that is required of him. Audience attention and involvement has to be sustained through the manner of the exposition:

> . . . interest and motivation should be sustained throughout by the use of material or examples which are intrinsically interesting to the

audience, dramatic, or simply funny. Concrete examples and stories make the material easier to assimilate, and should be subordinated to the main argument. (Argyle, 1972, p. 209)

(c) Voice

The voice is the means by which the exposition is transmitted and has to be loud and clear to be effective. The two most common problems about audibility are not being heard at the back of the room and not being heard at the end of sentences. Being heard at the back can be overcome by speaking to the back row and using eye contact to pick up the signals from those members of the audience sitting there. When they lean forward, cupping a hand to an ear or shake their heads at each other in bewilderment, you have a clear signal that there are problems requiring an increase in volume. The back row is also usually populated by awkward members of the audience; those anxious to slip out before the end and those least interested in the subject matter. Some hard-bitten exponents – like bishops and head masters – deploy the tactic of an opening question, "Can you hear me at the back?" delivered in a vigorous bellow to produce a whispered, "Yes", which is then followed by, "As soon as you can't hear, put a hand up or something". The members of the back row have then been stripped of the comfortable obscurity they were seeking and spend the rest of the exposition sitting nervously on the edges of their seats in case they are asked another question.

All speakers seem to have a natural tendency for volume to drop at the end of sentences, partly because they are running out of breath. In trying to overcome this difficulty there is the risk of the exponent becoming monotonous, as everything is on the same level, without any appropriate reference to the meaning of the words being spoken. *Pace* in speaking probably needs to be slowed down for exposition, as that of normal conversation is too quick for talking to a large audience of receivers. Also the speaking goes on for a much longer period without interruption, so that the exponent needs a slower pace to enable him to breathe and think. There is still the need to vary pace as a means of providing selective emphasis. There is also scope for *pauses*. These enable breathing and emphasis and help audience comprehension. They also provide a way of eliminating the nonsense words that frequently occur as someone is speaking:

> A recent gathering of mature men and women were listening for sixty minutes to a distinguished academic. Within fifteen minutes of him starting to talk, several members of the audience had stopped listening so that they could concentrate on the frequency with which he used the phrases 'in fact' and 'as it were'. Subsequent comparison

of findings showed that the rate was once every sixteen seconds and once every forty-seven seconds respectively. (Torrington, 1972, p. 87)

The reason for this type of distracting interjection is that the flow of ideas and the operation of the tongue are not correctly synchronised, so that meaningless words and sounds are produced occasionally to fill the void that the brain has momentarily left. Practice can replace nonsense words with pauses, which are better for the audience and for the exponent.

(d) Language
The language needs to be that which the audience will understand. The larger and more heterogeneous the audience, the more difficult for the exponent to cover that wide range of capacities. Marks (1980, pp. 54–60) has some helpful advice on this and points out how easy it is for professionals to slip into jargon that can puzzle many people, like the marketing manager to whom everything is a mix and the industrial relations manager to whom everything is a package. Few things can antagonise an audience more than the feeling that the exponent is trying to impress them with his cleverness rather than get his message across to them.

(e) Closing
At the end of the exposition the exponent summarises the points that have been made, reinforces them with the audience and leads the audience to some sort of follow-up action. That action may often be no more than to remember something of what has been heard, or to feel reassured, but it is the conclusion of the exposition that will lead into the action. The exponent has to avoid an anti-climax, which can be caused by signalling the end too clearly: "Let me sum up what I have been trying to say . . .". That both indicates that there is nothing new and confirms the view of the audience that it has not been well done. Instead the exponent aims for a climax – a positive close. Among the ways to do this are to tell a story, which brings together and illustrates the points that have been made; raising rhetorical questions to which members of the audience can now see answers where they could not at the beginning; and a straightforward statement which shows the interrelationship of points made earlier.

(f) Pitfalls
There are many things that an exponent can do wrong but the better he is, the more easily he can get away with them. The inexperienced

exponent should guard against some of the more common pitfalls, one of which is *apology*. If members of an audience are disciplining themselves to sit still and listen it will not make them more responsive to the exponent if he tells them of his incompetence. His best hope is to try and conceal it, rather than emphasising it. An example of an extremely apologetic opening is: "I cannot promise you that I have expert knowledge on this subject, so perhaps I may share with you some of my own confusion".

All of us can recall situations in which a speaker's *mannerisms* distracted us from what was being said. They are a form of displacement activity (see p. 33) and can not be restrained to the point of making the exposition wooden or stilted, but can be modified to avoid too much distraction. A common mannerism is walking about. In moderation this provides a mild variation in scene, but some of the more distracting variations are the walks that follow a precise, oft repeated path, to and fro, or those which include little flourishes like a slow motion, modified goose step. Standing still can be little better if it is accompanied by the act of balancing on the outside edges of one's shoes or using a toe to sketch, with great care and precision, a cross or triangle in the imaginary dust on the floor. Some exponents reserve for their expositions a minute examination of their fingernails or a series of isometric exercises to relieve muscular aches in their shoulders. Rings and bracelets are frequently played with incessantly, but the greatest distractor of all is probably the pair of spectacles that goes on, comes off, gets folded and put away, only to be taken out, unfolded, put on . . .

The problem of *not stopping* is that of the exponent who loses his audience by not stopping when he has finished, rambling from one anticlimactic afterthought to another as the audience chafes because the coffee will be getting cold. When you have said, "And finally . . ." you have no more than two minutes left. If you follow this with "To conclude . . ." and later, "As a last word . . ." and later still, "And this really is my last word . . ." you may excite sufficient wrath in the audience for them to start throwing things.

(g) Visual aids

We remember what we see for longer than we remember what we are told. Also we can sometimes understand what we see better than we can understand what we hear. This is the rationale for the use of blackboards, overhead projectors, films, closed circuit television, working models and experiments. They are, however, aids to, and not substitutes for, the exposition. Too much displayed material can obscure rather than illuminate what is being said. Television news provides a good example of how much can be used. The dominant theme is always the talking head with frequently intercut pieces of film. Very seldom do words appear on the screen and then usually as extracts from a speech or report, where a short sentence or passage is regarded as being especially meaningful. The other way in which words and numbers appear are when facts are needed to illustrate an idea, so that ideas like a change in the number of unemployed or the value of the pound sterling almost always have the figures shown on the screen to clarify and illustrate. Seldom, however, will more than two or three numbers be displayed at the same time.

Exponents need to remember the *size* of what they are displaying as well as its *complexity*. Material has to be big enough for people to be able to see and simple enough for them to follow. Material also has to be *timed* to coincide with what is being said. Where an exponent is using a display with quite a lot of information, it may be sensible to mask it and reveal one section at a time as the exposition proceeds, so that some members do not move on to a part of the diagram or table that has not yet been explained and which they do not yet understand.

6.1.3 Follow-up

The objective of follow-up is to reinforce the understanding that the members of the audience have developed through the exposition.

(a) Hand-outs
A typed synopsis of what has been said, or a copy of a diagram that has been displayed, can be helpful in reinforcement, but may reduce the level of concentration during the exposition itself. Furthermore some members of the audience will not read through the notes because they have just listened to what they contain.

(b) Measurement of understanding
For some expositions, like those used on induction courses, there is scope for checking understanding by members of the audience through using a questionnaire to test recollection of main points, but this is a rather threatening operation.

(c) Further meetings
If the exposition is one in a series of lectures, number two can reinforce number one by starting with linking material and continuing with occasional references back to earlier coverage. This is not only done in

expositions: how often have you been referred in this chapter back to earlier chapters? Another way in which further meetings can be used for reinforcement is if small discussion groups are to be run following an exposition, so that points can be picked up, clarified and developed further. This is the principle of briefing groups as well as the seminar in education.

References

Argyle, M., *The Psychology of Interpersonal Behaviour*, Pelican, 1972.

Bullock, A., *Hitler: a Study in Tyranny*, Penguin, London, 1969.

Marks, W., *How to Give a Speech*, IPM, London, 1980.

Marshall, P., *Mr. Jones, Meet the Master*, Peter Davies, London, 1954.

Mayerson, E. W., *Shoptalk*, Saunders, Philadelphia, 1979.

Torrington, D. P., *Face to Face*, Gower, London, 1972.

Chapter 7

Enquiry I:
The Selection Interview

Selection interviewing is rather like ballroom dancing in its heyday. The applicant depends on the control and direction of the interviewer, but most interviewers are as incompetent as the legions of tone deaf and flat-footed young men who trod so earnestly on the toes of their helpless partners during the quickstep, regardless of the immaculate rhythm that Joe Loss provided.

In ballroom dancing there has been a change as it has now become the province of the expert, who takes up the pastime because of genuine interest and some flair, and who is willing to train to reach an acceptable standard. This cannot so easily happen in selection interviewing as it is not easy to restrict the activity to trained enthusiasts. If the production manager is recruiting an assistant, he and the applicant have to meet and make a mutual assessment, no matter how incompetent the production manager may be at interviewing. Also there is no clear criterion of success in interviewing against which trainee interviewers can be measured. An apparent criterion is "getting the right person in the right job", but how can you judge when a person is right, and how do you know that others who would have performed better have not been turned away?

There has recently been a spate of books and training sessions for *interviewees*, seeking to improve their chances of success in job interviews by teaching them how to present themselves. These can only have limited value because control lies with the interviewer and our social conventions require the applicant to follow that lead, however ineffective the leader.

7.1 Ritual in Selection

Selection is one of the interactions where the ritual elements are most marked as the applicant is seeking either to enter, or to rise within, a social system. This requires the display of deferential behaviours:

> . . . upward mobility involves the presentation of proper perfor-
> mances and . . . efforts to move upward . . . are expressed in terms of
> sacrifices made for the maintenance of front. (Goffman, 1972, p. 45)

At the same time those who are already inside and above display their superiority and security, which are made the sweeter by the appearance of someone so obviously anxious to share the same privileged position.

Reason tells us that this is inappropriate and inhumane as it produces an unreasonable degree of dependency in the applicant; and the books (including this one) are full of advice to interviewers *not* to brandish their social superiority, but to put applicants at their ease and to reduce the status differentials. Even this, however, acknowledges their superiority as *they* are the ones who take the initiative; applicants are not expected to put the interviewer at his ease. Also the reality of the situation is that of applicant anxious to get in and selector choosing among several. It is not realistic to assume that the status differentials can be set aside. The selection interview is at least partly an initiation rite, not as elaborate as entry to commissioned rank in the armed forces, not as whimsical as finding one's way into the Brownie ring, but still a process of going through hoops and being found worthy.

7.2 Interview Effectiveness

If we turn to consider the reliability of the interview as a way of appointing the right people, there is the difficulty already mentioned of finding a satisfactory criterion of effectiveness. Many commentators, particularly psychologists with a penchant for precise measurement, have expressed the view that the interview is ineffective, for example:

> The bald conclusion from all the empirical evidence is that the interview as typically used is not much good as a selection device. (Morgan, 1973)

The main criticism is summed up by Webster (1964) after extensive research. He showed four main weaknesses:

(i) Selectors tended to decide for or against a candidate within no more than three or four minutes of the interview beginning. They then spent the rest of the interview looking for evidence to prove their first impression accurate.

(ii) Selectors formed tentative opinions on the basis of the application form and the appearance of the applicant; these were seldom altered by the interview itself.

(iii) When the selector has made up his mind, in the first few minutes, his subsequent behaviour betrays that decision to the candidate.

(iv) Selectors place more weight on unfavourable than favourable evidence.

The selection interview shows no sign of going away, probably because of its ritual significance, especially in appointments when promotion is involved, so the value of Webster's comments is to provide pointers of what to avoid. If the selector, for instance, is tempted to be unduly influenced by the initial impression that an applicant gives or gives off, he can reduce that tendency by self-discipline, even if he can not remove it altogether. He can also try harder to conceal his adverse opinion from the applicant. The easiest change is to shift the balance of evidence that is solicited away from the unfavourable towards the favourable.

7.3 Value of the Interview

Before examining the conduct of the interview, it is worth reviewing some of its potential benefits, despite the criticisms:

   (i)   The interview can be a key part in the process of deciding between different candidates for the same vacancy.

  (ii)   Applicants expect an opportunity to put their own case to a person or panel, rather than be judged entirely by objective methods.

 (iii)   The interview is an efficient way of clearing up points of factual uncertainty on both sides, such as clarifying exactly what the applicant was doing for two years in Peru or explaining the mysteries of the management development programme.

 (iv)   The interview is a logical conclusion of the employment process as information from a variety of sources – the application form, references, test results, the personnel specification and job description – can be discussed together and some assessment made of those intangible issues, like whether or not two people could work harmoniously together, that cannot be approached by any other way.

The interview is crucial in the employment process and when it is criticised for its unreliability, the criticisms do not constitute an argument for abandoning it: they constitute an argument for improving it. Apart from Webster, some of the most helpful research on interviewing is by Mayfield (1964), Lopez (1965) and Wright (1969).

7.4 Approaches to the Selection Interview

Selection interviews are sometimes conducted by panels of several people and in other situations it is a one-to-one discussion. The *individual interview* gives the best prospect for meaningful interchange, rapport, trust and efficient use of time, as there are only two trains of thought to be dealt with. It is likely that the applicant will find this process the easiest to cope with, as he is not having to adjust constantly to different questioners. This is the most common method in commercial and industrial employment. The drawback is that there is considerable dependence on the judgement of one selector, even though this may be mitigated by the use of a series of single interviews.

The *panel interview* is more common in the public sector of employment and is intended to ensure justice is done by requiring decisions to be made collectively by a group of people following discussion among them. It has the advantage that the decision is made quickly and there is no doubt that the ritual requirements are fully met, but does it produce sound decisions? The drawback is the inevitable inflexibility of the encounter and the overwhelming status differential of a panel sitting in judgement on the humble submission of a supplicant. There is little prospect of building rapport and developing a discussion; instead the applicant is fed a series of prepared questions, to which he offers answers that may also have been prepared. In one local education authority, for instance, the candidates are told beforehand the questions that they will be asked, so that the interview is really more like an audition as panel members sit silently appraising the performance. Because the panel members are so constrained, and perhaps apprehensive about the preferences their colleagues may have, the apparent "fairness" of the process is often suborned by attempts to get the decision effectively made before the interview, which is "only a formality". This suborning is done by informal interviews, one-to-one, beforehand, the exchange of confidential telephone calls to swap opinions and mild lobbying of panel members to ensure the appointment of Mr X.

Most selection interviews have one of three dominant modes. First is the *stress* interview, where the inevitable applicant anxiety is deliberately heightened by the selector to put him under pressure. This is usually justified by an idea that it will reveal weaknesses, demonstrating an orientation in the selector to look for the unfavourable, as Webster pointed out. Evaluating people's behaviour under stress is problematical and it is doubtful if it can be done adequately by other than skilled interviewers.

Opinion-soliciting is where the selector has a string of questions on which the applicant's opinion is sought – "Who should have final responsibility for negotiations with unions, personnel or production?" or "Which do you think is the better computer language, Fortran or Cobol?": the difficulty here is the same as with stress – how do you evaluate the evidence? How important are the opinions expressed by an applicant in a selection interview? He is predisposed to be sycophantic and can do no better than present ill-informed opinions, because he lacks knowledge specific to the post for which he is being interviewed. For posts where a particular set of values are seen as appropriate, applicants' opinions could be important and then detailed discussion would be necessary. It could be useful, for instance, to clarify an applicant's views on smoking if he was to be involved in advertising cigarettes, or his views on private education if his interview was for the headship of a school. Generally, however, this approach to the interview is only appropriate as a dominant mode when the interviewer is testing the applicant's technical *knowledge*. It is less suitable for testing understanding or ability.

The *biographical* approach is the safest and usually the most productive, as the discussion ranges over what the applicant has actually done. The objectives of this are clear, the progression logical and what lies behind the question is less open to interpretation, so that gamesmanship is reduced. The information already provided on the application form is enlarged and enriched as the selector builds up a full picture of what the applicant has done, and this is a more accurate way of deciding what sort of person he is than trading spontaneous value judgements or contriving artificial stress.

7.4.1 Preparation

(a) Selector briefing

The selector will brief himself by collecting and studying first the *job description*, which will have set down the details of the job to be done by the person appointed. Where there is no such document, he will either have to review his general understanding of what is required or ask someone. Secondly, he will look through the *personnel specification*, in which the ideal appointee is described, so that he has a picture of the job to be done and the sort of person envisaged for appointment. Thirdly come the *application forms* for scrutiny. We assume that there has been preliminary short-listing, so that there are only a few forms to consider and the interviewer will go through these checking for the congruence between what has been sketched in as the requirement within the

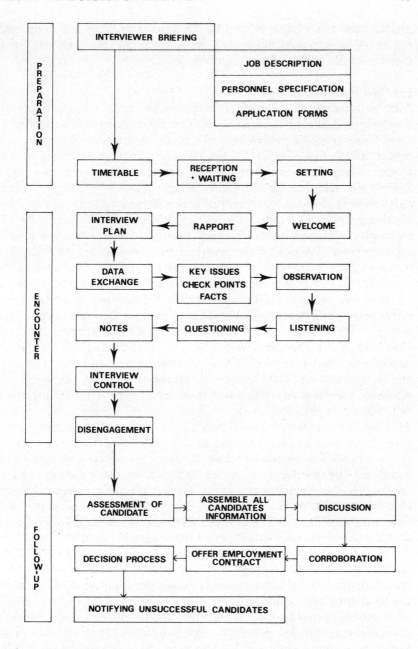

Fig. 7.1 A structured approach to selection.

organisation and what is offered by the applicants. This matching helps the interviewer to work out some ideas on the important points for clarification and discussion in the interview itself.

(b) Timetable

The importance of timetabling is to make sure that applicants are equitably and effectively dealt with. The rigid timetable can end interviews arbitrarily at a predetermined time and frustrate those involved or require another interview to be spun out for a further ten minutes, even though it has clearly finished already. At the other extreme, the highly flexible timetable can produce enervating periods of waiting by candidates. Nearly everyone reading this book will have had the experience of expecting an interview to start at, say, eleven o'clock and to be still waiting at 11.15 or 12.00. A junior hospital doctor seeking a post as registrar once commented that every minute you waited after the pre-ordained time reduced your ultimate life expectancy by a year. Some people regard this as an occupational hazard that applicants must put up with, like waiting for the dentist. He doesn't keep you waiting on purpose but sometimes he will be delayed because the previous patient is sick over the floor or grabs the drill and runs amok. Selectors are sometimes delayed in the same way. The flaw in this reasoning is that the dentist's patient has to do little after his enervating wait but sit in a chair and be operated on. The interviewee, on the other hand, has to *perform*: you want him in good, lively condition, not glassy eyed with fingernails bitten down to the elbow.

The best timetable is one which allows a break after each interview, with the applicants each arriving at different times. In most cases the selector has a few minutes to look through his papers and update his notes and the occasional interview can run late without any adverse effects. This arrangement also overcomes another horror, much beloved by some administrators, of asking all the applicants to arrive at the same time, so that Wilkinson sits for hour after hour as Adams, Evans, Jones, Phillips, Robinson and Smith are all dealt with before him.

(c) Reception and waiting

However much the selection process makes the applicant feel his worthlessness, he is still making up his mind. His acceptance of an offer of employment cannot be taken for granted and he will be looking for clues as soon as he enters the premises and will mildly quiz all those he meets before being summoned to "The Presence". Selectors may want to brief two intermediaries. One is the person on the door, who vets all visitors. Without briefing, this person may innocently confide to the applicant that everyone in the building is mad and that he personally cannot wait for the passage of the next thirty-two days, after which he is retiring, never to set foot in the place again, not at any price. That same person, briefed by the interviewer, can become a cheerful participant in the recruitment process by adopting a quite different attitude. The second intermediary is typically a secretary. "Take the lift to the tenth floor and his secretary will meet you". The hazards here are those who don't speak once they have identified the visitor, but press on with silent preoccupation through miles of corridors trailing the hapless applicant behind, and those who speak to everyone else but the visitor, clearly believing that the applicant is not really there at all. Briefing can produce not only a different attitude, but also some useful information – "When we get there I'll let you have a form for your expenses. Just post it back to me when you're ready". "They seem to be getting on quite well today. They've seen three people and there's one more after you". The selector might, of course, go to the lift himself so that the applicant's great uncertainty – what is the selector like? – is quickly done with.

Some time will be spent waiting for interview, although it will ideally be only a few minutes. In this time the applicant will want to compose himself and attend to what are known as personal needs. If he is going to wait for more than ten minutes he would almost certainly welcome at least the offer of a cup of coffee.

(d) Setting
It is difficult but necessary to combine two features of the setting for the interview: what is right for the ritual and what is needed to enable a full and frank exchange of information. Amiable chats over pints in pubs are not fitting for the seriousness of the selection enquiry, though dinners in exclusive restaurants are a different matter, for some odd reason. If it is a one-to-one interview, the following are the main aspects of the setting to consider:

1. The room should be suitable for a private conversation, free of interruptions.
2. It should be clear to the candidate where he is to sit.

7.4.2 Encounter

(a) Rapport
The opening of the encounter is when interviewer and interviewee make their preliminary mutual assessment. Details on method in rapport have

already been provided (see p. 43) but there are some points specific to the selection context.

A useful feature of the opening is to describe the procedure for the interview and its place in the total decision-making process. At the same time there is the opportunity for both to speak to adjust their mutual intelligibility and to feel comfortable with each other. The outline of the procedure gives the applicant a framework to settle into, as he hears what sort of interview to expect, how long it will take, whether he is to see anyone else, how the decision will be made and when he will know whether or not there is to be an offer. He will also hear that the selector knows what he is doing and will acquire a measure of confidence from that as well as the reassuring sound of hearing *himself* speaking.

(b) Interview plan

Assuming that the interview is not to follow the format of stress or opinion-swapping, the natural basis for the exchange is the application form. The information on it has been supplied by the candidate and is in some logical sequence, if the form is set out correctly. An important general question about forms is to check the purpose for which they are intended. Are they a basis for the employment record or are they a basis for the interview? Some forms still exist that are clearly drawn up with personnel records in mind. There are boxes in which applicants have to write their national insurance number, their local tax office, whether they have been vaccinated and the name of their next of kin. If, however, the form is designed as a basis for the interview or the selection process generally, then applicants will be asked to provide information which is relevant to the yes/no decision that dominates that process, so it will be in a logical form and usually in biographical sequence. It is probably not helpful to start automatically with the applicant's childhood and work steadily through each stage until the present, but some version of developing the conversation in a way that is sequential is helpful, even if this is going backwards. The best point at which to start is almost certainly the applicant's present job, ("Could you give me a general outline of your present responsibilities?") as it is both a question for which applicants will be prepared, and one on which they will be knowledgeable. Some suspicious selectors regard this as too vague and easy (what's wrong with easy questions?) and like to sharpen it up by saying something like, "I'd like to get a general idea of a typical day. What did you do yesterday, for instance?" The applicant will regard that as a question intended to tie him down and will try to break out of the restriction. In doing this he will begin to improve on the truth by switching in something that sounds good but happened last week, and switching out the hour yesterday afternoon when he slipped out to buy his wife's birthday present. The slippery slope of deception has begun already: the selector has turned the encounter into a battle of wits. Another shocking opening – but very common – is, "Why are you interested in this job?" That is threatening because the reasons for the application are often complex and not easy to summarise. Also they include reasons which applicants don't feel it is wise to declare, like more money, more power, longer holidays, an easier life and an opportunity to escape from the hopeless mess that they are making of the job they are in. The result is again deception ("Well, quite frankly, I'm looking for a bigger challenge. I feel I have more to offer than is required of me in my present post . . ."). It will have an element of truth in it, but will be exactly what the selector has heard everyone else say. Important elements of the plan will be key issues and check points. *Key issues* will be the main two or three features of the application form that stand out as needing elaboration or clarification. A particular episode of previous employment may need to be explored to see the range of responsibilities held, the number of subordinates, the difficulty of the circumstances. There may be key issues relating to education, experience in other countries or in specific industries that were noted by the interviewer in his preliminary briefing. *Check points* are matters of detail needing clarification: dates of an appointment, grades in an examination, rates of pay being some of the more common ones.

(c) Observation
Although the encounter will take the form of a conversation, information will not only come through what is said. The selector will collect some data by watching. Notes can be made about appearance, dress, height and weight, if these are likely to be important, and there will be at least some clues of change in the applicant's emotional state from his non-verbal behaviours.

(d) Listening
Although the interview is for the applicant to garner information as well as the selector, the applicant expects most of the information to flow *from* him as it is his opportunity to "sell himself". To do this he needs to talk, so selectors have to curb their own talking and concentrate on listening.

(e) Questioning
The various types and categories of questions are described in chapter 2, but the art of questioning depends upon the personality and style of the selector who will develop his personal technique through a sensitive

awareness of what is taking place in the interviews he conducts. Anstey describes this as the apotheosis of interviewing skill:

> Once rapport has been established, the actual questions matter less and less. The candidate senses what one is getting at, without worrying about the form, becomes increasingly at ease and responds more spontaneously . . . (Anstey, 1975)

(f) Notes

If notes are made on the application form they can be written around the information the applicant has already provided and are then easier to understand afterwards. Some selectors feel inhibited about taking notes in case it impairs the smoothness of the interaction, but all that seems necessary to prevent any difficulty is to develop a knack of jotting down points throughout the conversation without interrupting. The more one listens instead of talking, the easier note-taking becomes.

(g) Control

Remember the flat-footed ballroom dancer at the beginning of this chapter. The applicant will expect the changes to be controlled by the selector. It is for him to keep things moving, ensuring a brisk, business-like pace. He winds up discussion in one area and moves to another. He heads off irrelevant reminiscences and brings in the probes for matters that have been glossed over.

7.4.3 Follow-up

(a) Decision

After all the interviews, the selector or panel members decide to whom an offer will be made. They have not decided during the interviews themselves, if they remember Webster's criticism. Also they do not decide about individual applicants between interviews as that pre-empts the later interviews. The decision is made by the simple process of matching what is wanted (job description and personnel specification) against what is offered (information about individual candidates) and deciding on where the best match lies. There have been a number of attempts to put decision-making on a more systematic basis and many readers will be familiar with the classic works of Rodger (1952) and Fraser (1978) that have advanced schemes which have been widely adopted. It is not easy, however, to find evidence of these schemes being used in a disciplined way by contemporary interviewers. One recent piece of research

(Keenan, 1976) investigated the work of company representatives visiting British universities to interview third year undergraduates with a view to offering employment. The most important characteristic reported in the decision-making of these interviewers was "pleasant personality".

(b) Corroboration

When the decision is made there will be some corroboration of the *facts* that have been mentioned by the applicant. Customarily applicants do not wish their current employers to know of their attempts to find other employment so that they ask for the proceedings to be kept confidential. In that case the corroboration can only take place after the offer has been made.

It is difficult to see any justification for collecting *opinions* after the decision has been taken and the offer made. If this is to be done at all, the opinions should be collected before the interview or at least before the decision is finalised.

(c) Notifying the unsuccessful

The important thing is to let the unsuccessful know. A sizeable minority of employers do not bother and this not only seems unreasonable to the applicants, it also gets them a bad reputation in the labour market.

References

Anstey, E., *Techniques of Interviewing*, Barry Rose, London, 1975.

Fraser, J. M., *Employment Interviewing*, 5th edn, Macdonald & Evans 1978.

Goffman, E., *The Presentation of Self in Everyday Life*, Penguin, London, 1972.

Keenan, A., "Interviewers' evaluation of applicants' characteristics", in *Journal of Occupational Psychology*, **49**, 223–230, 1976.

Lopez, F. M., *Personnel Interviewing*, McGraw-Hill, New York, 1965.

Mayfield, E. C., "The selection interview: a re-evaluation of published research", *Personnel Psychology*, **17**, 239–260, 1964.

Morgan, T., "Recent insights into the select interview", *Personnel Review*, Winter, p. 5, 1973.

Rodger, A., *The Seven Point Plan*, National Institute for Industrial Psychology, London, 1952.

Webster, E. C., *Decision-making in the Employment Interview*, Industrial Relations Center, McGill University, 1964.

Wright, O. A., "Summary of research on the selection interview since 1964", *Personnel Psychology*, **22**, 391–413, 1969.

Chapter 8

Enquiry II:
The Attitude Survey

The common view of the attitude survey is the poll of electoral opinion or the questioning of shoppers about their brand preferences in super-markets. There are, however, many more applications in organisational life of this type of tightly structured interview. Examples are in job analysis and job evaluation, work study, training needs analysis and market research, as well as the assessment of employee opinion about prospective changes in working practice or payment arrangements.

The employment or selection interview is one aspect of enquiry, but the emphasis is on the single situation and the lone respondent from whom the selector is collecting enough data to put together a full, rounded picture of the candidate. In the survey interview the investigator is *sampling* a population and seeking data that is useful only in aggregate. The survey is to identify a relatively small number of pieces of information with emphasis on ensuring consistency of responses. This requires considerable preparation and discussion of exactly the question to be asked, including trial runs to test questions, and the development of a precise, unvarying structure. This inquiry technique is thus quite different from that of selection, even though it is concerned with information collection. The survey can predict quite accurately how a large number of people will respond in a given situation: which one of several possibles they will select as their member of Parliament, how they would respond to a change in the method of payment, how many would join a trade union if it were recognised by the management. It can also reveal dimensions of present behaviour that are not otherwise known: what people find most difficult in their jobs, whether they understand the payment scheme, whether they have confidence in their management.

Whatever the particular application, the common aim is *standardisation* of the information obtained:

> . . . the schedule standarized interview in which the wording and order of all questions is exactly the same for every respondent, the purpose being to develop an instrument that can be given in the same way to all respondents. All the questions must be comparable, so that when variations between respondents appear they can be attributed to actual differences in response, not to the instrument. (Denzin, 1970, p. 123)

One of the preconditions for accurate responses is that the respondent should feel confident in the neutrality of the inquirer, so that he will provide answers that are truthful and informative rather than answers that sound right but may be misleading:

> Managements who have carried out such surveys themselves have

frequently, and understandably, encountered bias in the answers they received from their employees, since the latter do not feel completely free to express their views. The survey is of little value unless such inhibitions are removed. Respondents must feel able to talk freely and frankly, secure in the knowledge that the results of the survey will be presented in such a way that complete anonymity is guaranteed. (North and Buckingham, 1969, p. 51)

Survey interviews involve more premeditation than others covered in this book as the interviewer is usually one of several, all trying to achieve consistency between each other in reporting.

8.1.1 Preparation

(a) Objectives
In deciding what the inquiry is to discover, we begin by considering what this form of inquiry *can* discover. Denzin (1970, pp. 123–124) lists four underlying assumptions:

(i) Respondents have a sufficiently common vocabulary so that it is possible to formulate questions which have the same meaning for each of them.

(ii) It is possible to find a uniform wording for all questions that is equally meaningful to every respondent.

(iii) For the meaning of each queston to be identical for each respondent, the sequence of the questions must be identical.

(iv) Careful pilot investigation, development and pretesting will provide a final schedule of questions that meets the requirements of the first three assumptions.

For the inquiry to be successful the respondents must, therefore, be a population with sufficient in common to meet the requirements of the first two of these assumptions. Also the information sought must be of the type that can be reduced to precise units of response to standard questions.

(b) The interview structure
The most detailed, practical advice for inquirers is in a booklet produced by the British Office of Population Censuses and Surveys and the following check list for drafting an interview structure is based on suggestions in that publication (Atkinson, 1978, p. 16):

(i) *What will be the respondents' reaction to the subject of the survey?* Responses to questions about payment arrangements are likely to be more guarded than responses on the (slightly) less sensitive topic of catering facilities.

(ii) *How can the subject be presented to respondents to achieve a high response?* In-company investigations are less likely to have problems with response rate than those conducted among the public at large, as the respondents are almost a captive population, but even a small proportion of refusals can reduce the reliability of the results.

(iii) *What is the best order in which to introduce topics?* Here we remember the principles discussed in the last chapter: the difficult and apparently threatening questions are put at the end rather than at the beginning of an employment interview. In a survey there is the need to begin with questions that are easy for the respondent to understand and reply to accurately, as well as getting him "on the wavelength" of the inquiry before proceeding to more complex questions.

(iv) *What wording of questions will produce precise data?* Here are the considerations of vocabulary and semantics with the need to use words that are not only unequivocal, but also where the meaning is not likely to drift with the respondent. Another consideration is the distinction between questions to obtain facts and questions to seek opinion. There is more on this topic in the section of this chapter dealing with the Encounter.

(v)   *How long can the interview last?* The need to know has to be balanced with the ability of the respondent to reply. Some respondents will not be available to answer questions for long periods, others will have difficulty in maintaining concentration and others will have much more to say than the interview schedule provides for. Also investigators may suffer from fatigue and lapses in concentration when repeatedly asking identical questions.

(vi) *What is the best layout of the survey forms?* Answers to the five questions above enable those organising the inquiry to prepare forms that are convenient for the inquirers to use in the variety of situations in which they are asking their questions.

(c) The pilot study

A pilot study tests the adequacy of the provisional interview structure. The interview is conducted with a small sample of respondents to test the various points on the above check list. Some words will be found insufficiently precise to stimulate the particular type of response that is needed. Certain topics will be more difficult and others easier than was anticipated at the planning stage. Timings will be monitored and – most important – the data collected will be analysed to establish that it is producing what is required. The number of interviews required for a successful pilot cannot be decreed out of the context in which the main study is to take place, but it will probably be necessary to pilot between 5 and 20% of the ultimate number of interviews required, depending upon the complexity of the survey and the eventual number of interviews to be conducted.

(d) Preliminary analysis

The results produced by the pilot are analysed in order both to modify the structure and to prepare the final analysis methods. The first is achieved by checking that the questions are producing the kinds of answer required and that there is no inconsistency between the results recorded by different investigators. The information received will also suggest additional questions because of potential in the inquiry that the designers of the structure had not realised earlier. This does not mean that the inquiry will be structured according to what the respondents want to say, but that ways of discovering information may turn out to be through different questioning approaches as well as through different wording of questions.

Preliminary analysis will require consultation with those who have sponsored the inquiry – key managers, a committee, a group of shop stewards or whoever it is who brought the inquiry into existence in the first place and who might call it off if developments are different from those anticipated.

Preliminary analysis prepares for final analysis by bringing in changes in the layout of interview forms to ease the collection of data from the forms and *coding* some of the responses whereby respondents are offered a range of alternatives from which they select one that is identified by a code number or letter.

8.1.2 Encounter

The dominant feature of survey encounters is their fleeting and anonymous nature. Two strangers meet as one asks questions of the other, with both knowing that they will soon part and forget each other. The transient and impersonal nature of the encounter leads to a degree of

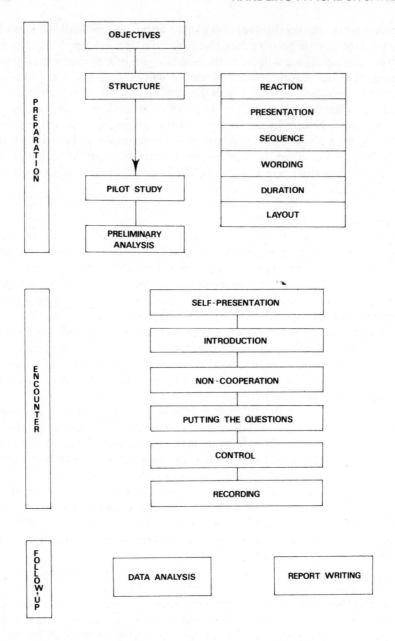

Fig. 8.1   A structured approach to the attitude survey.

frankness in answers that would be less likely if the respondent did not appreciate the quasi-mechanical nature of the investigator's participation and the fact that his own replies had no meaning other than as part of an aggregated, depersonalised accumulation of data:

> As an encounter between . . . two people the typical interview has no meaning; it is conceived in a framework of other, comparable meetings between other couples, each recorded in such fashion that elements of communication in common can be easily isolated from more idiosyncratic qualities. However vaguely this is conceived by the actual participants, it is the needs of the statistician rather than of the people involved directly that determine much, not only the content of communication but its form as well. (Benney and Hughes, 1956, p. 141)

(a) Self-presentation

The investigator has a strange part to play in this encounter as he needs to present himself positively enough to engage the attention of the respondent, who may initially be reluctant, at the same time as effacing himself to ensure the appropriate anonymity that the encounter demands. Those engaged to conduct surveys of public opinion are usually required to dress in a carefully calculated manner to emphasise their blandness and to de-emphasise their individuality. Denzin (1970, p. 140) offers a simple dictum:

> . . . dress in a mode of dress most acceptable to those being inter-viewed but employ a style that communicates who *you* are with respect to *them*.

(b) Introduction

Before the interview can begin the investigator has to provide certain information to get the respondent "in play".

  (i) *The purpose of the survey.* What it is intended to achieve and by what means. This will usually include comment on the authorisation of the investigation (e.g. ". . . the Works Council felt it would be helpful . . .").

 (ii) *How the respondent came to be selected for interview.* Sometimes in-company surveys cover all members of the prospective population who are willing to be interviewed, but usually representatives are identified and the respondent needs to know why he has been picked out.

(iii) *The confidentiality of the investigation.* The anonymity of the data has to be explained, especially if the interview is to begin with factual information that to some extent identifies the respondent. This is only to categorise the data, but it may seem to the respondent that he is immediately being personally identified.

(iv) *The fact that the respondent is a volunteer.* Respondents always have the opportunity to decline, even though the investigator may try to persuade him to cooperate. The unwilling respondent is of little value and usually gives distorted information because of his grudging compliance. If it is made clear that he is being invited to take part rather than being required to, then his compliance is more likely and his answers will be more helpful.

(v) *How long the interview will take.* This information should be accurate, so that the respondent thinks himself into the appropriate mode of response. If he thinks it will take five minutes, his degree of concentration will be less than if he thinks it will take half an hour.

(c) Dealing with non-cooperation

If it is true, as has been suggested above, that unwilling respondents are of no value, this might imply that the investigator accepts a refusal without comment and tries another respondent. The reasons for not being too passive are that the resulting information may not be truly representative of the population or that the refusal is based on misapprehension. Some people may be sufficiently timid or of such short service with the organisation that they feel their contribution would be of little value.

When there is initial reluctance it may be overcome by further clarification of the reasons for the investigation. If a reason for the refusal is offered, the inquirer has a basis for his further attempt. Some typical refusals and counters are:

Refusal	*Counter*
(i) "Well, I'm afraid I am rather busy at the moment".	"That's all right. I'll call again when it is more convenient. Would sometime tomorrow morning be all right?"
(ii) "I don't hold with all this survey business; it's a waste of time and money. My opinions are my business and no-one else's".	"Well, it is absolutely confidential, and I know that (they) are going to use these results quite fully".

| (iii) | "I've only been here a week, mate. Nothing I could tell you". | "We do need to get responses from people with all sorts of length of service. People who have been here for a few days notice things that others don't". |
| (iv) | "Oh, I don't know. Try someone else". | "We need to get as clear a picture as possible of what everyone thinks and your views would be especially helpful". |

Some of these will work most of the time, but not always. Other refusals are more confounding because they throw doubt on the care with which the operation has been planned:

"He's left".
"He's dead".
"It's Miss, actually, not Mrs".
"There's nobody called Warrington, but my name's Farrington".
"It's the first I've heard about it. They tell you nothing in this place.
" 'Consultation?'—they couldn't even spell it".

(d) Putting the questions
Suggestions here are again based on the comments of Atkinson (1978, p. 94).

(i) *Know the interview form.* The investigator needs to know the layout of the form before he begins and be able to scan forward from the question he is asking to those that are coming up. This produces a smooth sequence of question and answer without the personality of the investigator obtruding, and ensuring that the appropriate time is being allowed for each question.

(ii) *Put questions precisely as instructed.* They must always come in the predetermined order and using the standard wording so that variation in questioning is not a cause of varying data.

(iii) *Use linking patter.* Questions are probably grouped and the investigator needs to prepare respondents for the move from one group to another; otherwise the new question may be misheard due to the respondent still being on a different wavelength.

(iv) *Avoid assumptions about replies.* Investigators have to cope with the tedium of eliciting many similar responses, but there is a risk of assuming what the reply is without having actually heard it. If twenty people have produced an identical response the twenty-first may sound identical but in fact only be similar.

(v) *Use prompts to ensure consistency.* Prompting is a way of suggesting an answer and is sometimes built into the question itself, by offering an example of the sort of thing the question is looking for. On other occasions the investigator uses prompts to jog a person's memory. The important thing is that prompting should be done consistently and by prior agreement among interviewers.

(vi) *Watch for misunderstandings.* Sometimes respondents are so bound up with the answer they have just given that they misinterpret the next question and hear it wrongly, producing an incongruent answer. The usual way to deal with this is to repeat the question with as little overtone as possible. If the question is put again in another way there is the inevitable risk of distorting the response.

(e) Control and recording

The investigator has to control the encounter without having much flexibility, as he cannot stop before the form is satisfactorily completed and he cannot obtrude himself. He will often have voluble respondents who provide more information than is needed. In these situations he has to mention time limitations or make some flattering remark about the respondent's views being varied and interesting, providing a breadth of perspective that is very welcome, but at the moment there are some specific (not more interesting) questions to be answered. Where respondents produce answers that are incomprehensible, the investigator makes it clear that it is the investigator's naïvete and lack of experience that makes the answer meaningless. The respondent will then delight in making things clear to the novice.

An American study by Cannell *et al.* (1978, pp. 205–224) suggests the following features that affect the reliability of responses:

(i) *Time lapse:* as the time between an event and the interview increases, there is increased underreporting of information about that event.

(ii) *Salience:* events important to the individual are reported more accurately than those of less importance.

(iii) *Social desirability:* reporting of an event is likely to be distorted in a socially desirable direction.

(iv) *Event-specific recall:* characteristics of the respondent show considerably less relationship to reporting accuracy than do characteristics of the event being reported.

The same study produces evidence to support the view that reliability can be improved by reinforcing behaviours from the investigator, (e.g. "Thanks, this is the kind of information we want") and by getting the respondent to make an overt agreement to work hard at providing complete and accurate information. The latter sounds to this author like a strategy that would be more effective in the United States than in Britain, but the reader will make his own judgement.

Data from the respondent is recorded when it is provided; not recalled later. Many responses call for no more than a tick in a box or a circle round a number, so that the interviewer feels like a talking machine, but it is important to place the ticks and circles accurately. Where something is to be written in, it is written exactly as it is spoken: it is not paraphrased or condensed, although there may be a range of standardised abbreviations, like DK for "don't know".

8.1.3 Follow-up

(a) Data analysis

When all the interviews are complete and the forms gathered together, they are counted and sorted. Then the analysis of the data begins. The first stage is counting numbers and this is most likely a computerised operation as the straight data is picked up from the forms and fed into the machine for analysis and permutation.

(b) Report-writing

Having processed all the numbers, a report has to be written to show what the facts mean and how they are related. The information has to be understood and then explained in the report by means of a theory which makes sense of the data. The final, and crucial, stage of the report is producing some conclusions about future action which the interpretation of the facts illuminates.

References

Atkinson, J., *A Handbook for Interviewers*, HMSO, London, 3rd impression, 1978.

Benney, M. and Hughes, E. C., "Sociology and the interview", *American Journal of Sociology*, pp. 137-142, September 1956.

Cannell, C. F., Oksenberg, L. and Converse, J. M., "Striving for response accuracy: experiments in new interviewing techniques" in Ferber, R. *Readings in Survey Research*, American Marketing Association, Chicago, 1978.

Denzin, N. K., *The Research Act in Sociology*, Butterworths, London, 1970.

Ferber, R., *Readings in Survey Research*, American Marketing Association, Chicago, 1978.

North, D. T. B. and Buckingham, G. L., *Productivity Agreements and Wages Systems*, Gower, London, 1969.

Chapter 9

Problem-solving I:
Counselling

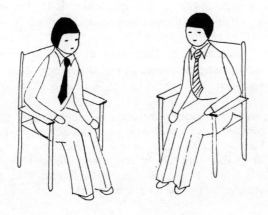

Counselling is a necessary management art which is little understood and rarely practised. People are just as likely to have knotty problems to solve at work as they are in other aspects of their lives. They will be uncertain about whether they are in the job appropriate to their interests and skills, whether they have prospects for change or growth in the job or in the organisation that meet their aspirations, and about whether their aspirations are known. They may have problems about job security, how they are getting on in the eyes of their superiors, whether they can cope with technical change and what may be involved in early retirement or redeployment.

There are often difficulties about working relationships within small groups and between superior and subordinate. Problems like these cannot be eliminated by counselling, but the ability of employees to cope with their surroundings can be enhanced by talking through their worry with a competent person; their adjustment becomes better and their contribution improves. That makes counselling a necessary management art; improving the fit between employee expectation of the organisation and organisational expectation of the employee. It is, however, an art little practised in Britain, although more widespread in the United States.

A definition of counselling by Pietrofesa *et al.* (1978) helps us to both understand the activity and see some of the differences between British and American practice:

> Counselling is a relationship between a professionally trained, competent consellor and an individual seeking help in gaining greater self-understanding and improved decision-making and behaviour-change skills for problem resolution and/or developmental growth . . . It is not giving tests, providing information, giving advice or gathering data in an interview. (p. 6)

The activity of counselling is gradually being professionalised, but there are very few professionally trained counsellors in the field of employment and even fewer in the ranks of management. Furthermore, it is less common in the United Kingdom than in the United States for people to seek this type of assistance. Counselling is typically provided spontaneously and informally without it even being acknowledged as counselling by the person seeking assistance, who will describe it as seeking information – perhaps advice – rather than seeking help in self-understanding. This general self-consciousness and diffidence means that counselling is generally disguised as something else. It may be a continuous feature of the working relationship between two people, it is more likely to come in an interview of some sort, either the semi-formal encounter of performance appraisal or the informal chat stimulated by an incident in day-to-day operations – "I think we'd better have a talk and try to sort this out".

9.1 The Counsellor as a Person

The extensive literature on counselling and its related research show that there is a "scientific" basis to counselling in that generally effective approaches can be distinguished from generally ineffective approaches, but the personal qualities and flair of the person who is counselling will be a greater determinant of success than any detailed understanding of the research.

> It is not difficult to teach someone who reflects positive counsellor attributes some basic counselling skills and produce an effective counsellor. On the other hand it is unlikely that one can teach helping skills beyond the most superficial to someone who is basically a non-helper. (Pietrofesa *et al.*, 1978, p. 37)

The most thorough analysis of the qualities that make an effective counsellor is by Combs *et al.* (1971) and includes the suggestion that counsellors need to be more concerned with other people than with things and events; that they are concerned about others and not merely with themselves and they see their role as being to encourage the process of search and discovery rather than working towards a predetermined solution to a particular problem. Above all counselling is an intimate, open activity and another reason why it is so rarely practised by managers is the fear of intimacy and of losing status or control in a situation through reducing the social distance between a manager and a subordinate. Also, many managers shy away from counselling because they feel they will not be successful. One quality that the counsellor has to demonstrate to the client is *respect*, accepting the client rather than disapproving of him, trusting him and being concerned for his welfare. This will be a part of the counsellor's philosophy, but it still has to be demonstrated:

> Initially the helper is most effective in responding with respect when he can be non-evaluative with the helpee. In addition, the helper

should encourage the helpee to express himself fully . . .
Respect is perhaps best communicated when the helper gives the
helpee his undivided attention and demonstrates that he is
committed to understanding. . . . (Gazda, 1973, p. 56)

Related to, but different from respect is *warmth*, creating a feeling of
safety and security for the client in his relationship with the counsellor. It
cannot be the easy intimacy of relationship with a close friend, but
neither can it be contrived:

. . . avoid effusive and chatty, buddy-buddy behaviour. The salesman's smile, handshake, and strained attempts to be friendly are the
antithesis of warmth. Instead the helper should immediately focus
on the needs of the helpee and begin to 'earn the right to care'.
(Gazda, 1973, p. 57)

Authenticity is an aspect of counselling that has received much
attention by the professionals, and Carl Rogers came near to believing
that it was the only quality that mattered in the counselling relationship.
The counsellor must be genuine not only in what he says and the
attitudes he displays, but also in the extent to which he discloses himself
to the client. This presents problems to people in management positions,
who sometimes feel that they have to dissemble or prevaricate in discussion with subordinates because of operational constraints on their
freedom to disclose information or their uncertainty about the reliability
of information ("It looks as if this person will be moved out of the
Marketing Department because of his poor performance, but it is not
settled yet. I can't tell him he will be shifted; I can't tell him he won't;
better not to say anything").

Empathy is a prerequisite of being able to help with the problems of
others in any more than the most superficial way. It has been defined by
Rogers (1951) as the ability of the counsellor

. . . to assume, as far as he is able, the internal frame of reference of
the client, to perceive the world as the client sees it, to perceive the
client himself as he is seen by himself, to lay aside all perceptions
from the external frame of reference while doing so and to communicate something of this empathic understanding to the client. (p. 29)

This is not quite the same as sympathy, where one is sharing the feelings
of the other and identifying with those feelings. This is not likely in the
relationship between managed and manager, but empathic behaviour is
easier.

9.2 The Counselling Process

The procedure for counselling varies slightly according to the theory one holds about counselling.

The most widely accepted mode of counselling is the *client-centred* approach, pioneered by Rogers in 1942. It is based on the proposition that all human beings have a need for positive regard and this can only be satisfied by others, so that the concept of self we all have is something we develop as a result of what we receive from others. If we then feel a need that conflicts with what we have learned from others, we are likely to categorise it as bad. Client-centred therapy is a way of enabling people to incorporate new experiences with what has been learned previously in order to acquire a more flexible concept of self. In this way there is a move towards self-actualisation, the prime motivational force in the individual. The counselling process is one of empathic understanding, in which the counsellor immerses himself in the world of the client, learning about it and enabling the client to understand it better by the process of sharing his experience and making explicit aspects of their world that were previously implicit and not truly known.

The specious appeal of this counselling approach to managers is that it is feasible for the lay person to adopt and comes close to normal every-day behaviour. Rogers made the comment:

> . . . the therapeutic relationship is only a special instance of inter-personal relationships in general, and that the same lawfulness governs all such relationships. (Rogers, 1961, p. 37)

Other theoretical approaches are less available to laymen either because of their dependence on high degrees of skill or because of their basis in a professional, doctor/patient type of relationship.

9.3 A Structured Approach to Counselling

Although, as has already been said, who the counsellor is is more impor-tant than counselling method, the following outline is offered as a way in which would-be lay counsellors can develop their own approach and style.

9.3.1 Preparation

(a) Counsellor briefing

Counsellors will have trouble if they start absolutely cold with a client, devoid of any information apart from knowing there is a problem. Clergymen and some social workers occasionally have to start in this way, but at least their position as counsellor is clear at the outset. In organisational life it is unlikely that anyone will be so clearly labelled, and the counsellor needs to have some prior briefing about the client. There may be some documents such as application forms or performance appraisals. There may be a background of knowing the prospective client through everyday working contacts or a series of telephone conversations with people who know him. The counsellor needs to be able to assimilate this material without reaching conclusions and deciding the outcome. If experience shows that prior briefing makes it difficult for an individual counsellor to avoid preconceptions he may prefer to begin with only the sketchiest of information in order to avoid distortion.

(b) Nature of the interview

How often do counselling encounters take place with both counsellor and client sharing the same perception of what the encounter is for? It must be the minority of lay counselling interviews that start like that. More often they will develop either spontaneously for both parties or at the initiative of one that was not expected by the other. The difficulty lies in the lack of acknowledgement in organisations of the value of counselling and its place in working relationships. Management Development Officers are not expected to initiate counselling interviews with trainees, they are expected to tell them how they are getting on. Employees do not expect counselling from their superiors, they may ask for information or advice.

In some circumstances a discussion between two people at work develops into a counselling event, but more often they are as the result of an intention by one person that has then to be shared with, and accepted by, the other. An example is the management trainee who feels disenchanted with the training scheme he joined a few months earlier and has rather vague ideas about what to do. He goes "to have a word with" the training officer, intending to resign, or to complain, to ask for a change or even to ask for a review of his progress. The training officer is then in the position of having to guess what the question means, due to the lack of a clear request for counselling. He has to decide whether there is a latent content to the enquiry other than the manifest content, as was described by Roethlisberger and Dickson (1939) in their early studies. They found frequent situations where a deep-rooted problem was signalled in an oblique way. Some managers go to extremes in injecting awesome significance into the most innocent comment, like the supervisor who would not accept that the request by a lady not to work overtime any more at the weekend meant just that, and was not a cry for help because her children had left home, her mother had died or her husband was beating her.

Another example is where a manager may be bothered about an employee's performance, lacking enthusiasm, turning in late for work, taking days off or whatever the symptom may be. He too decides he will "have a word with" the employee. Because of his authoritive position he will usually be seen as someone raising the matter as a preliminary to some form of punishment, inhibiting the likelihood of employee openness. To avoid the risk of client apprehension or defensiveness being too great, he is likely to conceal what he wants to talk about until the conversation itself begins.

Both these situations require the nature of the ensuing conversation to be shared and accepted by both participants before it can begin.

(c) Counsellor authority

The counsellor needs to be someone who can speak authoritatively. All the emphasis in the preceding few pages has been on counselling as a process whereby the individual improves his personal adjustment to his situation, so that the counsellor needs all those qualities of empathy, respect, warmth and authenticity which have been mentioned. When counselling takes place within the employment relationship there is the additional element that the counsellor needs to be in a position to take some action *on* the employment relationship. A typical outcome of this sort of counselling is some change in perception by the employee with a concomitant change in behaviour, accompanied by some changes in the work situation initiated by the counsellor and acting as reinforcers for the changes the client is making. He will be moved on to a different shift, given extra training, reassigned to less hazardous work or some similar action, without which he will himself do nothing.

For this reason the counsellor needs to be someone who can make that sort of change come about. He has to be worth talking to both in the sense of being able to make things happen to the context and enabling changes to take place in the context of the job. Another aspect of counsellor authority is his perceived competence in making judgements about the job. However non-evaluative the counselling approach, it is not so bland as to eliminate any evaluation at all. To some extent the straight opinion of the counsellor will be sought and will be needed. This requires understanding of the job the client is doing, other jobs in the organisation and the overall economic position of the organisation.

(d) Location and setting

The counselling interaction tends to take a long time. This is another reason why it is often avoided by managers. If it were professional counselling it might be protracted over several meetings, but that would produce an element of formality that would be inappropriate in organisational life, where there is seldom more than one session and a follow-up meeting to check on progress. For this reason the location needs to be one in which two people can have a private, uninterrupted conversation for a hour or more without arousing speculation about what they are up to. The nature of the encounter is going to be more informal than most of those discussed in this book and the setting should therefore help this informality:

> . . . eye-ball to eye-ball confrontation over yards of mahogany desk *may* help bolster your authority in a tough disciplinary interview, but for most purposes the interviewee will talk more freely if he is comfortably seated and can see the interviewer clearly without being obliged to stare straight at him. (Hackett, 1978, p. 17)

9.3.2 Encounter

(a) Rapport

The special nature of rapport in the counselling interview is that it determines whether or not the interview itself will take place. In selection, training or discipline rapport is needed to ensure a useful and effective interaction. In counselling it is needed to set up a sufficient degree of trust and understanding for anything to be done at all. Without it being done satisfactorily, the client may not disclose his concerns and commit himself to a frank exchange:

> Errors in understanding the client may result in his hasty withdrawal. And usually it is in this interview that the client decides whether the counselling relationship is the method he will use in his attempts to work out his difficulties. (Porter, 1973, p. 88)

Establishing rapport is therefore a longer phase than with other interactions. The counsellor will show his respect and warmth and will demonstrate his *attentive listening* to the client, as the client (rather than

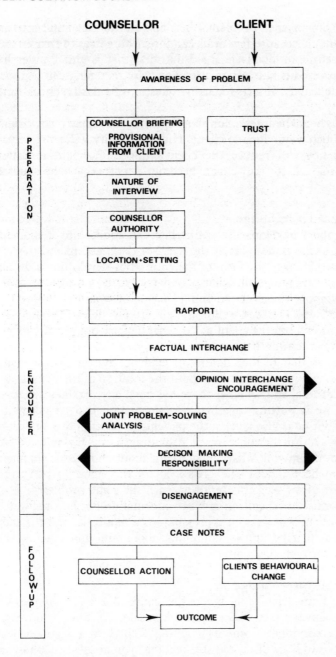

Fig. 9.1 A structured approach to counselling.

the counsellor or the "problem") becomes the focus of the interaction. This is difficult because few of us can forget ourselves to that extent and the confused, emotionally charged outburst that is either unleashed or being suppressed is not easy to attend to. Also, listening can be too keen, as when the listener inserts too many questions to clarify, check facts and so forth.

Throughout the interaction, but especially in rapport, the counsellor will *model* behaviour for the client. His equanimity will calm the client, his confidence will reduce the client's uncertainty and his attentive listening may help the client become attentive as the interaction proceeds.

(b) Factual interchange

As the rapport develops the counsellor can move into a more direct discussion of the issue lying at the heart of the meeting and the suggestion is that this takes the form of the counsellor developing a discussion that is a non-controversial exchange of data or facts, a review of what they both know about the situation and a sharing of what one knows but the other does not. The counsellor is deliberately deferring analysis and opinion; not inviting the client to say what he feels but putting together a data base for them both to use later.

This is similar to the eliciting of evidence by the doctor visiting a patient. As he puts his questions about the location of the pain, how long it has been there, and whether there has been any dizziness, sickness or diarrhoea, he is putting together the information that he needs for his diagnosis, but he is also getting the patient to reflect on his situation in a practical way. Furthermore he is providing some reassurance by the impression of knowing what he is talking about and by the fragments of information he provides—"There's a lot of this about" or "You're the fourth person I've seen this morning with the same problem".

The counsellor is collecting basic information on the situation about which the client will later be expressing his hopes or fears, he is showing to the client that he knows something about him and opening up the exchanges between them on a low key.

(c) Opinion interchange

The second interchange is when the counsellor and client exchange opinions about the facts. Usually the counsellor will move to this phase by inviting comment from the client—"Well, how do you feel about things generally?" or "But you still feel that you are getting a raw deal?" or some similar opener.

The importance of this stage is to avoid criticism of the client or decision-making about what is to be done regarding the issue being discussed. The matter is being opened up and understood by both parties. The counsellor is hearing the client's views, anxieties, apprehensions and hopes, so that he can build in his mind a fuller picture of what they are discussing, adding the opinions to the basic facts. The client is also coming to understand the matter better as he articulates his feelings. They have to be expressed, and thoughts have to be marshalled before they can be expressed. The unburdening helps to make clearer what his problem is.

The counsellor will mainly use the technique of reflection at this stage (see p. 51) rather than many questions, so that the client is helped to examine what he is saying and comprehend it more fully.

The direct input for the counsellor is to provide *reassurance* or encouragement, particularly if the client is being self-critical and showing a shortage of self-confidence. The counsellor may point out aspects of the client's job performance that are more positive and satisfactory than the shortcomings on which the client is tending to dwell. While avoiding the trap of patronising the client, he may be able to invoke positive comments that have been made by other powerful members of the organisation about the job performance. He may be able to say that no decisions have yet been made about early retirement or factory closure. Whatever the topic being discussed there will be some encouraging comments that the counsellor can make. This does not lull the client into a *false* sense of security; it helps to establish a *realistic* sense of security, after which some searching joint problem-solving can be attempted. In the job performance and working situation of every one of us there are some good aspects and some that are not so good. The objective of job counselling is to strengthen the good and modify the not-so-good, and a client will be more able to examine his situation constructively if the examination follows some reassurance and confirmation of his self-esteem:

> With all troublesome situations the counsellor provides a sense of hopefulness. This does not mean inappropriate or false reassurances. Hopefulness is a positive attitude that suggests there are solutions to most problems and that the manager is willing to invest some time in helping his subordinate find them. (Mayerson, 1979, p. 288)

(d) Joint problem-solving

There is now a shift of emphasis from the counsellor's encouragement to the client's analysis as the counsellor invites him to expand on the major features of the problem that have been opened up. The client is now moving away from "getting it off his chest" towards analysing his feelings and his situation, looking for causes and explanations. The initiative in analysis comes from the client, although the counsellor provides listening and understanding, with occasional questions and reflection to sharpen the focus and make connections:

> Helping the client to explore his situation more fully requires considerable skill and intuition. Nothing can be imposed on the client. He has to see any difficulty for himself, and to do this he needs to talk, with his talking perhaps aided by questioning and some focus from the counsellor. (Torrington, 1972, p. 60)

It is very tempting at this stage for the counsellor to get carried away by a desire to be helpful – and to get the interview over – by offering solutions. This is a particular problem for a manager, as his style of behaviour may be geared to making decisions for and about subordinates, and the client may be looking for this approach. The assumption underlying client analysis is that what the client says and understands he has begun to acknowledge and may be able to cope with, so that actions rooted in this analysis have a chance of working. On the other hand analysis produced by another – even a respected and respectful counsellor – may in some way or other be screened out by the client through cognitive dissonance. This is why the emphasis is on the client's own analysis. Part of the counsellor's contribution may, however, be to *confront* the client with the inconsistencies in his analysis.

It is in this stage of the interaction that the counselling succeeds or fails. Either the client breaks through to a fresh awareness of himself, his situation and what can be improved, or he remains unaffected and the remainder of the interview is an anti-climax with a further meeting being the only possibility of progress.

(e) Decision-making

Now counsellor and client work out tentative courses of action as a result of the analysis, with both of them having responsibility for implementation. They exchange opinions on solutions to the problem they have examined and gradually commit themselves to action. Some of the action will be taken by the counsellor, who can remove some impediments within the organisation or open up opportunities: some action will be taken by the client as he alters his behaviour in line with the changes to the working context that the counsellor is making.

The counsellor helps at this point to generate alternatives for the client to consider, arising either out of his experience and different viewpoint or out of his interpretation of the client's analysis. Another counsellor contribution is to agree targets with the client for getting things done, as a reinforcer for the agreed actions.

(f) Disengagement

Disengaging from this encounter involves attention to the future, so that any benefits from the exchanges are not lost. Apart from target-setting, the counsellor can review in detail what has been discussed to get the client's consent that they share the same understanding. Usually they will arrange a further meeting to check on progress.

9.3.3 Follow-up

(a) Case notes

If the counsellor makes some notes about the encounter there is a starting point for any other interaction that may follow and a reminder of the action that has been agreed. In some situations these notes can then be shared with the client so that an agreed version is produced. This has the advantage of confirming with the client what is going to happen and making the action less imprecise. The disadvantage is the extent to which the client will feel tied down by such a statement and find it inconsistent with the intimate, informal conversations that took place during encounter. With many clients the appropriate action would be made *less* likely if it were written up in a "contract" with the counsellor.

(b) Counsellor action

Client action will always be to change some aspect of his behaviour. Counsellor action can be more varied, depending not only upon the nature of the problem but also upon its deep-rootedness. The easy counselling interviews are those where the problem is resolved by the exchanges of the interaction itself: a misunderstanding is cleared or a piece of crucial information is provided. The counsellor will need to do little more in follow-up than produce confirmation. Where difficulties are more entrenched and require great effort by the client, the action by the counsellor will need to be more significant if it is to enable the client to be successful. Among the more effective counsellor actions might be changing the job the client is doing or to arrange for him to report to a different superior, as the job itself or the superior/subordinate relationship are the most common causes of problems at work.

References

Combs, A., Avila, D. and Purkey, W., *Helping Relationships*, Allyn & Bacon, Boston, 1971.

Gazda, G., *Human Relations Development*, Allyn & Bacon, Boston, 1973.

Hackett, P., *Interview Skills Training*, Institute of Personnel Management, London, 1978.

Mayerson, E. N., *Shoptalk*, Saunders, Philadelphia, 1979.

Pietrofesa, J. J., Hoffman, A., Splete, H. H. and Pinto, D. V., *Counselling: Theory, Research and Practice*, Rand McNally, Chicago, 1978.

Porter, E. H., *Introduction to Therapeutic Counselling*, Houghton Mifflin, Boston, 1973.

Roethlisberger, F. J. and Dickson, W. J., *Management and the Worker*, Harvard University Press, 1939, pp. 225–259.

Rogers, C. R., *Client-Centred Therapy*, Houghton Mifflin, Boston, 1951.

Rogers, C. R., *On Becoming a Person*, Houghton Mifflin, Boston, 1961.

Torrington, D. P., *Face to Face*, Gower, Farnborough, 1972.

Chapter 10

Problem-solving II: Discipline

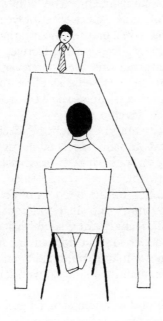

Many contemporary views of discipline are connected with the idea of punishment; a disciplinarian is one seen as an enforcer of rules, a hard taskmaster or martinet. To discipline school children is usually to punish them by keeping them in after school or chastising them. Disciplinary procedures in employment are usually drawn up to provide a preliminary to dismissal to ensure that the dismissal of an employee will not be viewed as unfair by a tribunal. This background makes a problem-solving approach to discipline difficult for a manager, as there is always the sanction in the background making it unlikely that the employee will see the manager's behaviour as being authentic in the sense used in the last chapter.

Despite the difficulties, this chapter is based on the more accurate notion of discipline implied in its derivation from the Latin *discere*, to learn and *discipulus*, learner. In disciplinary interviews the manager is attempting to modify the working behaviour of a subordinate, but it does not necessarily involve punishment. The aim of the interview is to achieve an adjustment of some aspect of employee behaviour to make it consistent with the objectives of the organisation. It is reasonable to argue that self-discipline is the most effective, as well as the most dignified, method of ensuring this consistency, and often it is the only means available. When there is self-discipline there is little need for supervisory controls and unless supervisory controls are withdrawn, self-discipline is not likely to develop.

There are three elements in a system of discipline. First there are rules and arrangements broadly acceptable to both employer and employee. These provide a framework of organisational justice to ensure general compliance with the rules because they are seen as worthy of support. This is a limitation on the freedom of action of managers, as it requires them to behave in a controlled and consistent manner. There will be many rules and arrangements, some formal and written down, some informal and understood. The formal are likely to include such features as rules about not smoking, punctuality and safety. The informal understandings will be mainly about conventions of behaviour and relationships.

The second element of the system is managerial control of individual and small group performance to ensure compliance with the rules and to correct deviations. The correct guarding of machinery by employees will normally be supervised, at least in the early stages of a person's employment while he is learning. The observance of times at which people start and finish work will be monitored, not only to obtain the employer's pound of flesh, but also to avoid dissatisfaction among employees about those who appear not to be abiding by the rules that everyone else is following. This control is only operated in relation to individual employees:

> ... whereas so-called group 'indiscipline' normally results from a widespread rejection of a working arrangement or rule and the resolution of any conflict lies in the negotiation of new work standards, individual indiscipline indicates merely a personal deviation from standards generally accepted by other employees. (Department of Employment, 1973, p. 2)

Managerial control of individual performance can only be exercised satisfactorily if there is a framework of rules, and the third element of the discipline system is only possible in the presence of managerial control. This latter element is what the other two are used to produce: self-discipline, or individual control of own performance to meet organisational objectives within a framework of organisational justice. It may seem that managerial control and individual control are not consistent. How can there be one with the other? The answer is that managerial control is needed to provide the learning that is a prerequisite of the self-discipline. The skilled craftsman acquires the autonomy and independence of his skilled status as a result of close supervision during his apprenticeship, and the sales representative acquires the freedom of the road after close schooling in the features of his product and the market in which he is to operate.

Even when someone is technically accomplished there may still be a need for managerial control. This is not the place to discuss the various theories of leadership, but the most accomplished performers in entertainment and the arts often lean heavily on a producer or conductor to enable them to produce the performance. In sport there are instances of a gifted player playing brilliantly under one captain and moderately under another. There is, therefore, some balance to be struck between managerial control and individual control. The manager, or monitor of performance, has to judge when to reduce supervision and by how much. In any occupation there is a proper area for external control – like quality sampling or the annual audit of the books – but there is also the area for self-control that cannot be invaded by the superior without jeopardising performance and impairing the manager/subordinate relationship.

More extensive consideration of discipline in employment can be found in Torrington and Chapman (1979, pp. 213–255), Megginson (1972, pp. 631–635) and the seminal article by Huberman (1964). This chapter is based on the assumption that the disciplinary interview is one in which the interviewer, who will be referred to as the *monitor*, is dealing with a situation in which there is a need for managerial control of individual performance, but not necessarily requiring a dressing down or rebuke. This may be needed, but until the monitor has determined what is causing the unsatisfactory performance he cannot know whether that is appropriate or inappropriate.

10.1 A Structured Approach to the Disciplinary Interview

10.1.1 Preparation

(a) Procedural position
With the unfortunate overtones of sanction that bedevil any disciplinary interview, the monitor needs first to check the procedural position.

In a minority of cases the likelihood of penalties will already have been set up by earlier interviews at which formal warnings may have been given. In that case the scope for problem-solving is limited as the procedural machinery has begun to grind inexorably, making further warnings or penalties difficult to avoid. Most interviews, however, precede procedure and the parties are less inhibited by procedural considerations. The monitor will need to emphasise the informality of the encounter, keeping procedural implications at bay. *In* procedure there is the likelihood of the employee being represented, *out* of procedure representation is less likely, although the employee may feel anxious and threatened without it.

(b) Evidence
Disciplinary interviews always start at the command of the management, so the monitor will need to collect his evidence before he begins the encounter. This will include some basic details about the respondent, but mainly it will be information about the aspects of the working performance that are unsatisfactory and why. Too often this exists only in opinions that have been offered and prejudices that are held. This provides the monitor with a poor basis for a constructive interview, so he needs to ferret out details, with as much factual corroboration as possible, including a shrewd guess about the respondent's view. It is almost inevitable that the respondent will start the interview feeling that he is being blamed and he will therefore seek to refute any allegations. He will look at the matter from his own point of view and deflect blame else-

where. This will often be necessary, but the monitor needs to predict what sort of reaction he will meet and brief himself to deal with the reaction as well as with facts aligned with the comments of his managerial colleagues. Unless the impending encounter is at an early, informal stage, the monitor also needs to know about earlier warnings, cautions or penalties that have been invoked.

(c) Participants

Who will be present when the encounter takes place? The most obvious person is the one whose contribution or organisational objective is being doubted. If he is to be tried and sentenced in his absence there is no need for an interview, so his attendance is inevitable. The more difficult question is whether or not he will be accompanied by a representative. The monitor will usually feel it better if there is not such representation at an early, informal stage on the grounds that the presence of a representative makes the proceedings more formal and denies the flexibility of discussion and problem-solving that a one-to-one encounter would offer. The respondent, on the other hand, may feel so vulnerable if he is confronted behind closed doors that he would want to be represented as soon as there was a whiff of discipline in the air. If he does feel vulnerable and insecure, the presence of a "friend" or representative may provide the degree of confidence that is needed for him to be able to look at his situation in a problem-solving rather than defensive way.

Once an interview takes place *in* procedure, the monitor will be more willing for the employee to be represented, especially if it is a procedural requirement.

What is the role of witnesses? Many disciplinary interviews involve the monitor dealing with a matter reported by others and perhaps depending upon verbal evidence. The foreman says the respondent hit him and Frank saw him do it. Do Frank and the foreman come to the interview in case the respondent claims that the foreman started it and Frank wasn't looking anyway?

If the interview is well into the formal stages of procedure, it may well be necessary for the witnesses to be produced with all the problems of charge and counter-charge and the difficulty of determining whether the respondent is more sinned against than sinning. Before that stage is reached the monitor will do better to handle the matter alone, but he will need to work on the basis of more tangible evidence.

(d) Location

The appropriate location will also vary according to the formality of the proceedings. The early, informal discussion designed to solve a problem

before it deteriorates into opposed attitudes and rigid procedure needs an
environment similar to that of counselling, to provide the opportunity of
empathy and demonstrated respect. The further the situation moves
towards sanctions and the possibility of dismissal, the more appropriate a
stiff, formal atmosphere becomes. It is not authentic behaviour for a
manager to invite an employee into his office, provide a cup of coffee and
a cigarette, and then say in a warm and friendly tone of voice with
accompanying smile and eye contact: "By the way, I think I ought to tell
you that you are being dismissed on Friday. I'm really most terribly
sorry." That sounds ludicrous but is only a slight exaggeration of what
can happen as managers try hard to be liked in spite of the bad news they
are delivering. No amount of "niceness" in the way news is conveyed will
make more acceptable what is being said, and the wrapping up in
honeyed words may make the stark truth hard to understand. Unusual
formality is appropriate for the later, judicial phases of disciplinary
procedure and the large, impressive offices of senior managers make good
Star Chambers.

10.1.2 Encounter

(a) Explaining the management position
The encounter is taking place because of management dissatisfaction
with the employee's performance. The employee is probably dissatisfied
himself, and this will become clear in a good encounter, but the starting
point is the management dissatisfaction so the encounter begins with a
statement, by the monitor, of that dissatisfaction.

The statement is of *facts* about an operational problem; it is not a
statement of disapproval or moral outrage about the facts, as the monitor
is dealing with a problem and not—yet, at least—dealing with an indolent
or disobedient employee. Whether there is blame to be attached to the
employee has yet to be determined. If, for instance, a man is being interviewed about unpunctuality it is not appropriate for the monitor to begin
by telling him that his behaviour is reprehensible—"Your timekeeping
this week has been disgraceful . . ."—as it might be that the man had a
seriously ill child needing constant attendance through the night, and
this would make the monitor's behaviour reprehensible. A more even-
handed opening statement—"Each day this week you have been at least
twenty minutes late . . ."—is a more effective opening as it concentrates
on the problem without allocating blame and it is a reasonably precise
statement of the facts that is not likely to lead to an argument about
values. It also sets a limit on the dissatisfaction as it specifies only one

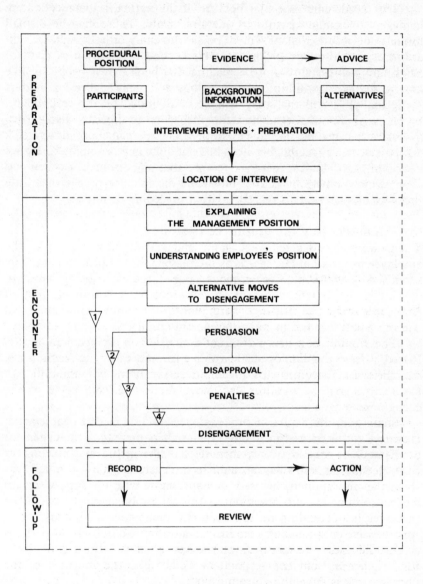

Fig. 10.1 A structured approach to discipline.

issue, implying that there is no other problem. If there are other problems, they should also be mentioned.

This needs emphasis first because of the normal reluctance among managers to handle disciplinary matters firmly. There may be a small minority of people in management posts who enjoy brutalising their subordinates, but they are probably as far beyond redemption as Captain Bligh and will certainly not be reading this book. Most people dislike having to take up disciplinary questions and tend to broach matters ineffectually, fearful that they will be confounded by the respondent. Secondly there is a tendency for managers to initiate disciplinary measures because an employee simply "doesn't come up to scratch". There is nothing specific, but he is just not quite good enough. "Can't we get rid of him?" Unless there are reasons that one can make explicit and about which something can be done, the disciplinary process has little prospect of success: it is merely a ritual preceding dismissal.

(b) Understanding the employee position
There are two sides to every story and the monitor now asks the employee to say what he regards as the reasons for the problem and how seriously he views it. The employee is not therefore being asked to explain *himself* but to comment on the problem. It is unlikely that all employees will make that nice distinction in their minds, but some will and most will respond to the difference in emphasis.

The monitor now gets a different dimension on the problem, as it is looked at from the employee standpoint. In most cases the reaction is a straightforward account with the employee explaining why the difficulty has arisen, and the monitor can move on to the next stage of the encounter.

Sometimes the nature of the employee reaction can be problematic. He may, for instance, not understand when there is a management problem. Why should twenty minutes lateness in the morning matter when he stays an extra half an hour in the evening? Why so much fuss about the ripe language he used in conversation with the supervisor? In his last job that was commonplace. Another problem can be when the employee is not willing to talk about the matter at all, because he is apprehensive or anxious to keep his private affairs to himself, or perhaps because he does not want to implicate anyone else. A third difficulty is angry defiance from the respondent as he feels the injustice of the situation that is developing around him.

(c) Examining the problem
After these first two stages in the encounter, the monitor will have

reached the point where the respondent knows that there is management dissatisfaction about a specified aspect of what he has done, and the respondent will have explained his point of view on the problem described. Now is the time to move towards a solution, with action by the monitor, by the employee or by both. As in counselling, it is not realistic to view the encounter as one that ends with all the follow-up action being taken by the respondent, who proceeds to behave himself instead of mis-behaving. It is just as likely that some management action is needed to remove an impediment.

If a local van driver is developing the habit of being drunk during the late afternoon, one solution is for him to stop drinking during the day, another might be to dismiss him forthwith, but a third might be to change his duties to fork-truck driving inside the factory where it is less likely for him to be able to drink on duty. If another employee is con-stantly arguing with a supervisor and questioning orders he receives, one solution would be for him to stop being disobedient, but another might be to shift him to another job where the relationship with a different supervisor would be less abrasive and help him to develop compliant behaviour. A familiar argument against this type of reasoning is that managers should not have to pander to employees in this way. Going to work involves some inconvenience and places obligations on employees that have to be met, and employees not able or willing to meet these obligations should make way for someone who can and will.

That is a statement of how people *ought* to behave, according to a particular point of view. If, however, there is a problem about the work-ing behaviour of an employee that can easily be overcome by a small administrative change, it seems worth doing, especially if it is a problem that the employee cannot otherwise resolve. If managers are going to take the time and trouble to conduct problem-solving interviews on disciplin-ary issues it is realistic for them to go one step further and see if there is some practical step that can be taken either to enable the employee per-formance to alter, or to reinforce some resolution on a change that the employee may make as a result of the encounter.

The process of clarifying the problem and "holding it up to the light", as it were, so that both monitor and respondent can see it and look at it from different angles, may be enough to produce the solution. Both parties agree on what is to be done and agree to do it, so that the encounter can move to a conclusion. *This is the first possible move to disengagement.*

(d) Dealing with the unresponsive respondent
Clarifying the problem may be enough to produce a solution to it, but if

the respondent will not respond to it, there is now a test of the power behind the monitor's managerial authority. There are at least three further steps that can be taken one after the other until one of them is effective. In some situations steps one and two have to be omitted, with the monitor moving directly to the third.

(i) *Persuasion*. The first step is to point out to the respondent that there are aspects of what he may want to achieve that will not come about unless his behaviour alters:

> "If your output doesn't meet the standard by the end of the training period, your earnings will drop".
> "Good timekeeping is an absolute must for anyone wanting a transfer into Inspection".

If the respondent comes to see that it is in his own interests to alter what he has been doing, that is one form of powerful inducement. *This is the second possible move to disengagement.*

(ii) *Disapproval*. Some people are more concerned to propitiate others than to pursue their own best interests, so they may respond to a suggestion that their behaviour is displeasing those whose goodwill they wish to keep:

> "The Management Development Panel are rather disappointed . . .".
> "Other people in the department feel you are not pulling your weight . . .".

Alternatively the monitor may take it all upon himself:

> "This simply is not good enough in a competitive industry like ours . . .".
> "If this happens again, it will certainly be a formal warning, and the next step would be dismissal".

This is the third possible move to disengagement.

(iii) *Penalties*. If all else fails, or if the other possible moves to disengagement prove to be inappropriate, penalties have to be used. This will be either with an obdurate employee or when there is a serious offence about which there is no doubt. The most common penalty is the formal warning that comes as a preliminary to possible dismissal, but other possibilities are relocation or demotion, which move the respondent to a job that is less attractive than the one he holds. Suspension with or without pay removes the employee from his employment for a short period without terminating the contract. All of these are penalties that fall short of dismissal. In situations that are sufficiently grave, summary dismissal is both appropriate and feasible within the legal framework. *Penalties represent the final possible move to disengagement.*

(e) Disengagement

The move to disengagement may come at any one of the four points mentioned above. How does the monitor handle the close of the encounter? In some ways the easiest situation is summary dismissal as the employment relationship is going to end and the only considerations are of the procedural fairness and administrative accuracy with which it is done, so as to reduce the possibility of a tribunal hearing.

If the outcome of the encounter is anything other than dismissal the close needs to do what it can to make the return to the workplace as positive as possible. The employee who slinks out with shoulders slumped and spirit humbled may satisfy the occasional bloodthirsty manager, but will be ill-fitted for resuming his duties if these require him to be poised and self-confident.

10.1.3 Follow-up

(a) Record

Except for the most informal encounters a record of the discussion has to be made by the monitor, not only to have a note of what should happen, but also for procedural reasons:

> After the disciplinary interview is over, it is essential to record both the fact that it has taken place and a synopsis of what transpired. Thus if the interviewee has been officially reminded during the interview that the consequences of further offences will have to be considered in terms of the further stages of a disciplinary procedure . . . he should be given a copy of a permanent record of the fact that this was said. (Hackett, 1978, p. 154)

Even when the juggernaut of procedure is not involved, there is still value in noting what was agreed in order to reduce the likelihood of a difficult matter being conveniently forgotten.

(b) Action

Something must happen after the interview. Some managers seem to believe that it is enough to demonstrate that they were right, rather like getting the better of someone who challenges you to a duel, but the point of the exercise is not to prove you were right, it is to bring about a change in the working performance of the respondent. There is also the possibility that interviews in procedure result in the matter going further as the respondent appeals against what has been said and any penalty that may have been given to him. If there *is* an appeal the importance of the written record becomes even greater.

(c) Review

Some time after the interview the matter has to be reviewed to see what has changed. Has the problem been overcome or is there still a difficulty? If all is well there may be a need to review any warnings, especially formal warnings, that the employee may have received, as procedure often includes provisions for "cleaning the slate" of an employee who has been in trouble but manages to put matters right after a trouble-free period. The last aspect of review is to consider disciplinary problems in aggregate. If certain types of problem occur frequently with different people, there is need for further investigation. Also rules need regular review to ensure that they relate to current aspects of operations rather than those that are obsolete. Recently a small brewery reprinted its works rules, containing several instructions to employees about horse-drawn vehicles but none about motorised vehicles, although they have not used horses for thirty years.

References

Department of Employment, *In Working Order: a Study of Industrial Discipline*, HMSO, 1973.

Hackett, P., *Interview Skills Training*, Institute of Personnel Management, London, 1978.

Huberman, J., "Discipline without punishment", *Harvard Business Review*, August 1964.

Megginson, L. C., *Personnel: A Behavioural Approach to Administration*, Irwin, Homewood, Illinois, 1972.

Torrington, D. P. and Chapman, J., *Personnel Management*, Prentice-Hall, London, 1979.

Chapter 11

Conflict Resolution I: Negotiation

Negotiation has become a much more commonplace activity in recent years as more traditional methods of settling arguments have become impracticable. In international affairs, open warfare between states has been partly replaced by negotiation; terrorism has introduced negotiation as a necessary method of dealing with hijackers and others who have taken hostages; leaders of political parties negotiate uneasy alliances with each other to provide a basis of government; and business deals proliferate.

Although a long-standing art, negotiation has developed as a major mode of decision-making, even though the development carries with it the feeling that it is a poor substitute for executive action. Henry Kissinger, the American Secretary of State when the protracted negotiations to end the Vietnam war were completed, said:

> A lasting peace could come about only if neither side sought to achieve everything that it had wanted; indeed, that stability depended on the relative satisfaction, and therefore the relative dissatisfaction, of all the parties concerned. (Kissinger, 1973)

In employment we have acquired the institution of collective bargaining as a means of regulating the employment relationship between employer and organised employees. To some this is the cornerstone of industrial democracy and the effective running of a business, but to others it is seen as impairing efficiency, inhibiting change and producing the lowest, rather than the highest, common factor of cooperation between management and employees. Norman Tebbitt was appointed Secretary of State for Employment in the British government in September 1981 amid expectations that he would be "tough with the unions". On his first day in office he expressed a view probably echoed by many, when he said:

> I never believe you can compromise on difficulties. They have to be openly faced and you cannot just smudge them away with smooth words. (Tebbitt, 1981)

Is negotiation rightly viewed as an activity that is only second best to unilateral decision? If the outcome is no more than Mr Tebbitt's compromise, then negotiation may be the recourse of no alternative other than capitulation. In that situation some would argue that capitulation by one side would be a better outcome for *both* than a compromise that smudges the difficulties and dissatisfies both. There is, however, an alternative to splitting the difference in negotiation and that is where the differences in objectives between the parties are accommodated to such an extent that the outcome for both is better than could have been achieved by the unilateral executive action of either.

Any negotiation is brought about by the existence of goals that are common to both parties and goals that conflict. If the Egyptians and Israelis had not had at least one common goal (to stop fighting) the Camp David talks to find a settlement between the two countries could not have taken place; if they had not had a number of conflicting goals, the talks would not have been necessary. Between employer and employees the desire to keep the business in operation is one of the goals they usually have in common, but there may be many that conflict, and the two parties negotiate a settlement because the attempt by one to force a solution on the other would either fail because of the other's strength or would not be a workable solution without the volition of the other party. Both parties acknowledge that they will move from their opening position and that sacrifices in one area may produce more-than-compensating benefits in another. Many years ago the American Homans expressed the situation thus:

> The more the items at stake can be divided into goods valued more by one party than they cost to the other and goods valued more by the other party than they cost to the first, the greater the chances of a successful outcome. (Homans, 1961, p. 62)

Another limited view of negotiation is that the encounter is merely to disclose what each party wants to the other and that the outcome can be predicted beforehand: "They will ask for 10% . . . we will say 'no' and six weeks later we'll settle for 5%". Where that happens the negotiations are locked into a pattern of no more than compromise, whereas they should be approached as a process that *shapes* the outcome, as the parties explore possibilities of integrating their conflicting objectives. This can be a long, time-consuming process, it is often accompanied by acrimony and mistrust, but it is a way of introducing significant change and overcoming problems that cannot be dealt with as well by other means, providing that the nature of the process is understood:

> . . . negotiators seek to increase common interest and expand cooperation in order to broaden the area of agreement to cover the item under dispute. On the other hand, each seeks to maximise his own interest and prevail in conflict, in order to make the agreement more valuable to himself. No matter what angle analysis takes, it cannot eliminate the basic tension between cooperation and conflict that provides the dynamic of negotiation. (Zartman, 1976, p. 41)

The main work on understanding the negotiating process is that of Ann Douglas (1962), which has been the basis of more recent work in the UK by Morley and Stephenson (1970, 1977), Brotherton and Stephenson (1975) and Kniveton and Towers (1978). A complementary strand of analysis was developed by Walton and McKersie (1965) as well as a rather different approach by Walton in 1969. In all of these we find an approach to negotiation which describes it as a constructive process, whereby differences between parties are openly confronted and there is then a working towards an accommodation of the differences to provide a degree of satisfaction for the objectives of both parties which is greater than can be achieved either by simple compromise or by the "victory" of one.

11.1 The Bargaining Setting

Negotiating is such a specialised activity that it needs appropriate circumstances to make a productive outcome likely.

(a) Resolution or accommodation?
The parties in negotiation are confronting differences between them: dealing with *conflict*. This does not by any means involve violence, nor is it necessarily bitter and combative, but it is a divergence within the co-operative framework. That may be *resolved*, in which case the original feelings of opposition disappear and the relationship between the parties becomes one of cooperation without any element of conflict. This has obvious attractions and many people feel that negotiation has failed if resolution is not achieved. We must, however, recognise that many of the matters negotiated in the field of industrial relations are those where a conflict of interest is inevitable. Management representatives are mainly seeking efficiency, cost-effectiveness, productivity and the obedience of others to their own authority. Employee representatives are seeking high pay, freedom of action, leisure and scope for the individual. To some extent it is inevitable that these will conflict, so resolution of conflict may be a viable objective that can seldom be achieved. More realistic is an *accommodation* between the diverging interests, whereby the differences persist, but a way of living with them is found. This sounds like an unambitious objective, but an accommodation can still introduce major change in the workplace and a new situation which is both better than the one it replaced and better than could have been achieved by the unilateral

action of the management. Negotiators need to consider the alternatives in their initial target-setting and decide which they are hoping to attain.

(b) The balance of power

Negotiations only begin because each party has some power over the other. Naturally each team of negotiators wants to be the one with the power advantage, but it is doubtful if this helps them. If there is an imbalance of power it is difficult for *both* parties to be frank and to trust what is said by the other. The weaker party will be defensive and suspicious, lacking the confidence of having some room for manoeuvre. The stronger party will feel inhibited from destroying the opposition. The best situation is where there is an equality of power between the two.

In the ebb and flow of economic prosperity there come times when management have considerable power in relation to their employees and are in a position to say "no" to claims without too much fear of short-term inconvenience in industrial action. Usually they take advantage of such situations to bring about changes despite employee reluctance, and often economic stringency leaves then with no alternative. On other occasions the employees' union representatives are in a position to make substantial demands because their position is relatively stronger and the management have less freedom of action.

Only a dreamy idealist would argue that they should not use the power when they see the opportunity, but the short-term gain may become a long-term handicap: revenge is sweet. This argument – that power parity is most conducive to success in negotiations – only holds while there is a negotiating relationship. Managements may be able to use periods of the odds being in their favour to remove some matters from negotiation altogether. This chapter began with the assertion that negotiation *has become* a much more commonplace activity in recent years. The apparently indefinite period of high unemployment in the future, coupled with the social and technological changes that accompany it, may be bringing in an era in employment where the nature of management/union negotiation will undergo a permanent change in significance.

(c) Tension level and synchronising

A negotiating approach by one party to the other is best made when the other party is ready to deal with it. Managers often resort to negotiation only when there is no alternative due to a crisis having developed, making a negotiated solution the only possible outcome. It may not be a propitious time for the employees, so that their response is grudging or

ill-prepared, involving procrastination. The next time the management
may not be prepared for an employee initiative, with similar results.

The timing of most negotiations is dictated by extraneous factors
rather than the inclinations of the negotiators, but those involved have
some influence on the timing of encounters and may be able to push them
towards a time of mutual readiness. One aspect of appropriate timing is
the level of tension that exists. If this is too low there is no real will to
reach a settlement so that negotiators do not have the impetus to grapple
with difficult questions. If there is too much tension, there is so much
anxiety that negotiators cannot see issues clearly and become pre-
occupied with interpersonal wrangling and vilification. If negotiations
can take place when both sides have a balanced desire to reach a settlement, this can be as helpful as a balance of power.

11.2 A Structured Approach to Negotiating

Ritual is especially important as negotiation is a specialised activity and
its conflictual base makes for formality and awkwardness rather than
relaxed, informal behaviours. All confrontations have strong ritual
features. The international tennis player "shows" the new balls to his
opponent even though they both watched them being produced from
the box; in some Arab countries it is impossible to make any major
purchase without drinking tea; in the nineteenth century duels between
young aristocrats were fought according to a most elaborate set of rules;
and management/employee negotiations are also full of ritual steps. This
infuriates some newcomers to negotiation, who see it as time-wasting
prevarication, but it is an inescapable feature of the process, even though
it may not be a feature of other similar activities like consultation and
providing information. The rituals make a structured approach to
negotiating, in the manner of this book, particularly appropriate.

11.2.1 Preparation

(a) Agenda
The nature of the agenda can have an effect on both the conduct and
outcome of the negotiations. It affects the conduct of the encounter by
revealing and delimiting the matters that each side wants to deal with. It
is unlikely that other matters will be added to the agenda, particularly if

negotiations take place regularly between the parties, so that the negotiators can begin to see, before the meeting, what form the discussions can take.

The sequence of items on the agenda will influence the outcome of negotiations as the possibilities of accommodation between the two positions emerge in the discussions. If, for instance, all the items of the employees' claim come first and all the management's points come later, possibilities do not turn into probabilities until the discussions are well advanced. An agenda which juxtaposes management and employee "points" in a logical fashion can enable the shape of a settlement to develop in the minds of the negotiators earlier, even though there would be no commitment until all the pieces of the jigsaw were available.

Many negotiations take place without an agenda at all, sometimes because there is a crisis, sometimes because neither party is sufficiently well organised to prepare one, and sometimes because the party initiating the negotiations believes there is some tactical advantage in surprising the opponent. Morley and Stephenson (1977, pp. 74–78) review a number of studies to draw the conclusion that agreement between negotiators is facilitated when there is the opportunity for them to experience "orientation" – considering on what to stand firm and on what to contemplate yielding – or an understanding of the issues involved. An agenda is a prerequisite of orientation.

(b) Information and objectives

Although negotiations sometimes seem to be nothing but opposed opinions and heated exchanges between strong personalities, the currency of the exchanges and the basis on which a case is made or refuted is information, so that negotiators prepare by marshalling and mastering data. The information is needed first to understand the situation and the issues that are the subject of negotiation, and secondly to review the party's position – its strengths and weaknesses. This may throw up the need for further information. When the information is collected the negotiating team need to meet to ensure the same interpretation among them of that information.

The objectives of the negotiators will be partly set down in the agenda, and collecting and sharing an interpretation of the relevant information may have to precede work on the agenda to make sure that it reflects correctly what the negotiators are trying to achieve.

Seldom do management negotiators work out useful objectives. This may be due to a distaste for the whole bargaining activity, but often it is because the only outcome they can see to the encounter is to lose something, and their objective is to lose as little as possible. In recent years the question, "What do you seek to achieve in the forthcoming negotiations?" has been put to those entering both real and laboratory-type negotiations. Very seldom is the answer clear and reflects only vague values, usually because the question is such a surprise:

"Show them who is in charge".
"Assert management authority".
"Get the best deal we can"
—and the ubiquitous,
"Play it by ear".

When they can approach negotiations with some objectives that amount to more than a simple negation of what is sought by the other side, then there is the opportunity of finishing up with a mutually satisfactory agreement. Unless both parties want something out of the meeting there is little scope for anything but mutual attrition.

The objectives will not all be achieved, but their reality will be improved by predicting the counter-claims. This is not simply what is on the agenda as topics for discussion, but the nature and expected strength of the arguments that will be heard. If a team of negotiators can guess what will be said to them, they may well be able to restructure their objectives to stand a better chance of success in meeting them. This does not necessarily mean seeking less, but it probably does mean seeking differently: possibly more.

(c) The negotiating team

The attention of all negotiators will be directed towards handling the differences *between* the parties. Differences *within* parties are a nuisance, so that the team that is not united not only serves poorly the interests of those they represent, the time of those they oppose is also wasted, as the opponents do not know who is to be relied on. It is therefore important that the members of each team agree among themselves first, so that the two opposed sets of interests can be accurately confronted.

Atkinson (1977, pp. 87–89) suggests that there are three basic functions of a bargaining team: negotiating, recording and analysing, and that teams should comprise people to handle these separately. Another way of looking at team composition is to consider the roles of the participants, while accepting that there are quite different activities to be undertaken. The major role is leading spokesman or *advocate*. This is the person who will set out the team's case on each succeeding point, examine the opposing case and make a series of on-the-spot judgements about when to introduce new material, change tack and all the other decisions that shape the quality and direction of the encounter. The advocate has the lion's share of the negotiating task to perform, and is likely to be the person with the most status among the team members. If another member of the team were seen clearly to out-rank him, there would be a tendency for the opposing team to appeal to this more senior member, thereby undermining the effectiveness of the advocate and the cohesion of the team.

The *specialist* is the team member who does not lead, but who deals with particular points of information and analysis that may occur. In talks on payment arrangements, for instance, there may be a specialist to answer questions and provide facts about how the existing pay scheme works, or to correct false impressions that may be claimed. There may be several specialists, or some who come only for certain phases of the negotiation. They are not involved directly in the debate and negotiations are not helped by the single shop steward who advances a separate line of argument, nor by the manager who begins to make points that detract from rather than support the case that is being mounted by his advocate. Negotiating does not benefit from free-for-all, unstructured discussion.

There is no need for all those present to speak, even though many people feel that they have to justify their presence by speaking and get progressively more embarrassed as time goes by and they have not yet said anything. There is a valuable part to be played by those who simply *observe* as they have two advantages over other participants. First they do not suffer the same degree of agitation and hurt that attends those who suffer the "slings and arrows" of heated argument. Secondly they do not have to cope with the job of preparing what they are going to say and making their entry into the dialogue. That means that they hear more of what is said on both sides and are able to assess developments more dispassionately than the advocate, who is too busy, and the specialist who is interested more in one aspect than others. When there are adjournments it is the observers who can best initiate discussion among team members as strategy is redefined and further tactics considered. Observers can also record proceedings, although it is often only the outcome that is worth recording rather than the discussions themselves. Observers are most conveniently people of equal or junior rank to advocates and specialists. When someone attends who is perceived as a potential overrider of decisions or knocker-together of disagreeing heads, it makes the negotiations a hollow process if he never speaks.

A possible additional role is that of *chairman*. The logic here is clear, but the practice usually different. Logically one cannot act simultaneously as judge and counsel for the prosecution, so that one person is needed to chair the discussion and control the meeting, while another engages in advocacy. In practice, most negotiations seem not to need chairing, because the proceedings are discussion or argument rather than debate. There is a fairly rapid change of speakers from one side of the table to another, usually involving only one person, so that chairing becomes irrelevant. In larger, more complex negotiations it is more common to find a chairman. Usually it is a member of the management, other than the advocate, sometimes there is a convention that the chairmanship alternates between the two sides.

11.2.1 Encounter

(a) Setting
We saw in chapter 2 that there is a preference for face-to-face orientation between people who are engaged in a competitive task. Negotiations are best conducted when the seating arrangements divide the parties clearly as this focuses the attention of everyone on what issues divide them, and it is those issues that have to be understood, juxtaposed and eventually accommodated. Other aspects of seating arrangements are summarised by Kniveton and Towers (1978, p. 56):

> . . . participants vary in status and tend to select positions which reflect this status. Secondly, the position selected affects the influence the member has over the meeting, and thirdly, the seating arrangements affect the flow of communication.

The highest-status person in each team would normally be in the middle seat on his side, although Kniveton and Towers make the interesting comment that a principal negotiator hoping to dominate the meeting would tend to take the head of the table, but would take a different position if he was wanting the other side to take the initiative.

The number of people taking part in negotiations has two main influences. The first is in the preparatory discussions, when strategy is being formulated and cohesion being developed; the second is in the negotiating encounter itself. Slater (1958) conducted experiments from which he concluded that the optimum size for discussions of the type that precede negotiation is five. If there are fewer, group members may feel that they lack variety or expertise or do not discuss the issue forthrightly because of an overwhelming desire to be nice to each other. If there are more, the scope for individual participation is reduced by the number of competing voices. In negotiations themselves the number of active, vocal participants will be less, but everyone will be communicating in some way, even if only by periodically raising their eyebrows or biting their

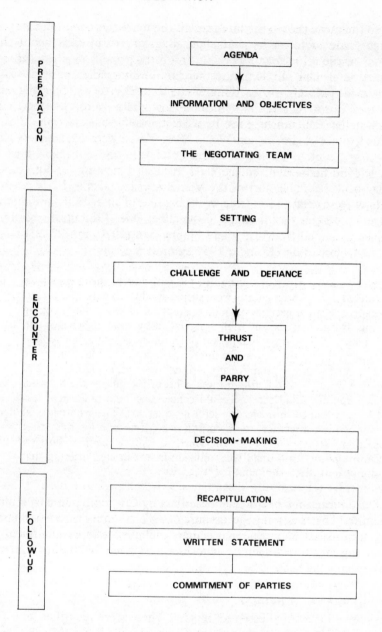

Fig. 11.1 A structured approach to negotiation.

nails, so the more people that are present the more there is a tendency to a distant type of formality and a puzzling variety of cues about the reactions of the other team.

Because of their public nature there are innumerable examples from international political negotiations of the difficulty that the setting can present. Winston Churchill described how there were two levels of activity at the Teheran meeting between himself, Roosevelt and Stalin towards the end of the Second World War. There were plenary sessions with thirty people present and "three-only" meetings between himself, Roosevelt and Stalin, with interpreters. It needed meetings of both types to make progress. The start of the Vietnam peace talks in Paris twenty years later were delayed for three weeks because of an inability among the negotiators to agree on the shape of the table! One of the most beguiling examples is quoted by Morley and Stephenson (1970, pp. 22–23) from Harold Macmillan describing a 1955 summit meeting:

> The room in which we met filled me with horror the moment we entered it. The protagonists were sitting at tables drawn up in a rect- angle; the space between them was about the size of a small boxing ring. But this arena was itself surrounded by rows of benches and seats which were provided, presumably, for the advisors, but seemed to be occupied by a crowd of interested onlookers. The walls were decorated with vast, somewhat confused, frescoes, depicting the end of the world, or the Battle of the Titans, or the rape of the Sabines, or a mixture of all three. I could conceive of no arrangement less likely to lead to intimate or useful negotiations. The whole formal part of the conference was bound to degenerate into a series of set orations. It was only when the Heads of Government or Foreign Ministers met in a small room outside in a restricted meeting that any serious discussion could take place.

If restricted meetings of the type described by Churchill and Macmillan are required in industrial negotiations, it not only alters the character of the main negotiations, it also makes more difficult the representative role of the employee spokesmen, who may be seen as being "in the management's pocket".

(b) Challenge and defiance
Negotiations have three essential phases. These were identified by Ann Douglas (1962) and more recently corroborated by Morley and Stephenson, working on British rather than American situations.

The first phase is described here by the melodramatic term "challenge and defiance" to acknowledge the theatricality and quasi-warlike nature of the first ritual step in the dance. Advocates set out the position of their parties and reject the position of the other, so that by the end of this phase members of both teams should clearly understand what the issues are that divide them, why, and how extensively. This differentiation is a necessary preliminary to the integration and problem-solving that follows. An important feature of the antagonism here is that it is between the *parties*, not between the individual negotiators. This is partly to emphasise the strength of their case, which lies in the power of those they represent. Few individual managers see themselves as being more significant and persuasive as individuals than as members of a larger body like "the management" or "the board", so that in most situations they add weight to their statements by alluding to their collective strength:

> "The Board are right behind me on this one . . .".
> "All my colleagues agree . . .".
> "The management position is perfectly clear . . .".

Employee representatives similarly emphasise their representative role:

> "Feeling on the shop floor is very strong . . .".
> "We have a mandate from our members . . .".
> "The membership has spoken . . .".

Another reason for the partisan emphasis is that there is a realisation on both sides that they will move at some stage later — otherwise there is no point in negotiating — and the movement later can be consistent with an early assertion of absolute immovability only if the early statement is attributed to the party that is represented and the later movement is initiated by the people sitting round the table.

The other reason for this stage is a simple stiffening of the sinews and summoning up the blood, as the negotiators hear their case spelled out for the first time in public and realise how well it is organised and how just it is. They thought they were right, now they know it.

(c) Thrust and parry

After the opening show of strength the differences are known and some idea of the relative strength of the parties is beginning to form in the minds of negotiators. There is then an almost instinctive move to the next, integrative stage of the encounter. The term "thrust and parry" is used here to describe this essentially quicker and inter*personal* stage as negotiators seek out possibilities of movement and mutual accommodation. The assertive emphasis of challenge and defiance is replaced by more tentative comments, more listening and more direct response to what is being said by others. Negotiators sound out possibilities, float ideas, ask questions, make suggestions and change the style of the encounter towards a problem-solving mode. The tentative nature of the proposals is maintained by the way in which they are contrasted with what was said earlier. Challenge and defiance is "official" and authorised by the parties. Thrust and parry is "unofficial" without any authority—yet. Thrusts are couched in non-committal terms, specifically exonerating the party from any responsibility:

> "My colleagues here will probably crucify me afterwards for saying this, so please don't take it as a formal offer, but suppose we could . . .".
> "We have no mandate from the membership, and I don't know whether they would wear it or not, but . . .".

These behaviours are not false in the sense that negotiators are simply revealing what they have already agreed beforehand; as has been said earlier in this chapter, that is the model of compromise. The negotiating process itself shapes the outcome of the encounter being described here, so the non-committal behaviour of the negotiators is quite genuine as a variety of possibilities is explored.

Gradually the opportunities for mutual accommodation can be perceived in the background of the talks.

(d) Decision-making

The *target point* of a negotiating team is its declared objective that was spelled out so positively in challenge and defiance. The *resistance point* is where they would rather break off negotiations than settle. This is not declared, otherwise it would immediately become the resistance point, and it is often not even known by the negotiating team, as the point at which they *would* resist is seldom the same as that at which they think they would resist. Throughout both challenge and defiance and thrust and parry the resistance points of both parties will have been moving to and fro as different possibilities become apparent. The third phase is when they reach an agreement.

It is usually up to the management to make an offer, although sometimes the employees have to take that initiative. What to offer, and when to offer it, is the single decision that is the watershed of the negotiating process and requires supreme judgement to get it right as it has two immediate effects. First it destroys the management target point, replacing it with the new offer. Secondly it will have an effect on the resistance point of the employees.

The offer may be revised, but eventually an offer is made that the employees will accept and the encounter is complete, although the negotiations are not.

11.2.3 Follow-up

(a) Recapitulation
When the agreement has been made the tension of the encounter is suddenly released and bargainers want nothing more than to get out of the negotiating room and spread the good news. If this temptation can be resisted, there is benefit in recapitulating the points on which agreement has been reached so as to ensure that there is no misunderstanding and to pick up any minor matters that have been overlooked. If they are picked up at this point they should be dealt with speedily because agreement is in the air. If they are left over for another meeting they will stand on their own and may be more contentious.

(b) Written statement
It is foolhardy for the negotiators to split up before a written statement has been agreed. It can only be brief, and may well need to be expanded later, but if a statement is agreed before the meeting ends, then all subsequent understanding of the agreement reached—by the negotiators themselves and by others—will be based on that statement rather than word-of-mouth accounts that are likely to alter so much in the retelling. Remember how "Send reinforcements, we are going to advance" became "Send three and fourpence, we are going to a dance". Until the agreement is written down, it will rest on an understanding, and understanding can easily change. There will be enough trouble in interpreting the agreement without adding to it by having a variety of agreements to interpret.

(c) Commitment of the parties
Although agreement has been reached, it is so far only between the representatives of the two parties and is of no value until and unless the parties themselves accept it, and make it work. Employee representatives have to report back to their memberships and persuade them to accept the agreement which consists of something different from what was in the original mandate. Management representatives may have to do the same thing, although they customarily carry more personal authority than employee representatives.

Only when the parties are committed is the deal complete.

References

Atkinson, G. G. M., *The Effective Negotiator*, Quest Research Publications, London, 1977.

Brotherton, C. J. and Stephenson, G. M., "Psychology in the system of industrial relations", *Industrial Relations Journal*, pp. 42–50, Autumn 1975.

Douglas, A., *Industrial Peacemaking*, Columbia University Press, New York, 1962.

Homans, G. C., *Social Behaviour, Its Elementary Forms*, Routledge & Kegan Paul, London, 1961.

Kissinger, H., report in *New York Times*, 25 January 1973.

Kniveton, B. and Towers, B., *Training for Negotiation*, Business Books, London, 1978.

Morley, I. and Stephenson, G. M., "Strength of case, communication systems, and the outcome of simulated negotiations: some psychological aspects of bargaining", *Industrial Relations Journal*, pp. 19–29, Summer 1970.

Morley, I. and Stephenson, G. M., *The Social Psychology of Bargaining*, Allen & Unwin, London, 1977.

Slater, P. E., "Contrasting correlates of group size", *Sociometry*, **21**, 129–139 (1958).

Tebbitt, N., report in *The Guardian*, London, 17 September 1981.

Walton, R. E., *Interpersonal Peacemaking*, Addison-Wesley, Reading, Mass., 1969.

Walton, R. E. and McKersie, R. B., *A Behavioural Theory of Labour Negotiations*, McGraw-Hill, New York, 1965.

Zartman, I. W., *The 50% Solution*, Anchor Press/Doubleday, New York, 1976.

Chapter 12

Conflict Resolution II: Arbitration

Arbitration is resolving conflict between two parties by the judgement of a third. In negotiation we were examining an activity where the outcome depends on two parties finding an accommodation of their opposing points of view by their own efforts. In arbitration that initiative is passed to a single person or panel, recognised as independent by the participants, who "hands down" a decision about the matter that the parties are obliged to accept.

There can be difficulties about the perceived independence of the arbitrator. If there is a disagreement between an employee and his supervisor, the employee may feel that a more senior manager arbitrating in the matter will inevitably be prone to favour the supervisor. It will probably be the only recourse for the employee, and the senior manager will at least be a different person from the one against whom the grievance lies. Also the process of arbitration draws the arbitrator towards an impartial position.

Another difficulty can be the unwillingness of one party or other to accept the decision that has been made. No arbitration can be guaranteed sound before it takes place, so that dissatisfaction of one party or other is likely. Judicial systems typically provide the opportunity of appeal against a judgement, although only a small minority of cases ever go to appeal, but arbitration in industrial matters is less likely to provide that course. An important prerequisite is the willingness of the parties to seek arbitration in the first place. If it is a voluntary step by both, there is a commitment to accepting the judgement when it is made and it is difficult to reject it because it is unpalatable. The art of the arbitrator partly lies in avoiding a judgement which is a total agreement with the case of Party A at the expense of Party B or vice versa. There is usually scope for some reconciliation of the opposed positions. Not only does this reduce the degree of potential dissatisfaction with the outcome, it may also find a more mutually satisfying solution than the two parties could find unaided. There is a limit, however, to the initiative that an arbitrator can take in proposing novel solutions, as he would be binding the parties to proposals that might be unworkable. The arbitrator can never have enough detailed understanding of the working situation to impose new methods that can be guaranteed reliable in practice. That may be possible for the *mediator* or *conciliator*, who are also third parties trying to resolve conflict between two others, but their mode of operation is different. The mediator chairs discussions between opposed parties and helps agreement to be made around the table. The conciliator is the envoy who shuttles between the opposing camps trying to get them to understand the point of view of each other. In both those interventions the agreement is freely made by the parties. In arbitration the decision is made by the third party and imposed on the others: it must be workable, so the arbitrator must be cautious. The best-known form of arbitration in the field of employment is in the work of the Advisory, Conciliation and Arbitration Service:

> If a dispute cannot be resolved by conciliation, ACAS may, at the request of one or more parties to the dispute, but subject to the consent of all of them, refer it for settlement to an independent arbitrator or arbitrators or to the Central Arbitration Committee (CAC). There is no legal compulsion on the parties to accept an arbitrator's award but, in practice, arbitrators' decisions are almost invariably accepted. (ACAS, 1980, p 82)

Some industrial relations agreements make provision for independent arbitration as the final step of an internal grievance procedure, and there are some examples of third-party intervention over a long period to "facilitate problem-solving and negotiation in dispute areas" (Margerison and Leary, 1975, p. 3). Also there are many cases, day-by-day, where people in management posts have to "sort out" feuds and squabbles between staff members. Mostly these are brief, heated exchanges that erupt because two people can't get on together, but sometimes a situation develops over a long period and a series of misunderstandings or more substantive problems have to be dealt with. All too frequently such matters are dismissed as "failures of communication" or "personality clashes", implying either that all that is necessary is more information or that resolution is not possible because the parties dislike each other. In fact there are often useful possibilities for arbitration to improve working relationships by more thorough means than increasing information and despite people's likes and dislikes.

This chapter has something to say about all these varieties of arbitration.

12.1 A Structured Approach to Arbitration

12.1.1 Preparation

(a) Arbitrator orientation

Arbitrating is not a commonplace activity, so the arbitrator may have to think himself into the situation beforehand and consider what the other participants will be expecting from the encounter. The disagreeing parties will look at the issue from two different *frames of reference*. This may be difficult for the arbitrator to remember, however obvious it sounds, as he is trying to establish some objective reality. Although his intervention may induce modifications in the opening positions of the two parties, their approach will be with different values, priorities, hopes and fears.

The parties will also both be seeking *justice* in the sense that they are wanting to be proved right. They will seek confirmation of their actions by someone of higher status, not only to get their own way in a disagreement, but to be able to claim justification for what they have done. In some serious disagreements the desire for justice may extend to wanting the other party to get his come-uppance, so one aspect of justice is to have oneself proved right and the other is for the opposing party to be proved wrong and, perhaps, to be punished in some way. A common example here is where a rank-and-file employee may want his foreman not only proved wrong, but to apologise as well, knowing that the forced apology will be a humiliation for the foreman.

If two parties go to arbitration the disagreement between them becomes a major issue. Not only will they be looking for justice being declared as on their side, they will also take with them a great fear of loss of *face*. The more firmly committed to a position you become, the more difficult it is to abandon, so that the arbitrator is faced with a difficult problem that has become more intractable by his very involvement.

(b) Roles

There are at least three different roles in an arbitration encounter. The most important is that of the *arbitrator* himself. This is the term that will be used in this chapter although the activities are sometimes very similar to those of the mediator.

On assuming office all British magistrates take an oath in which they swear to:

> ". . . do right to all manner of people after the laws and usages of the realm without fear or favour, affection or ill-will."

That rather optimistic statement is the type of *independence* to which the arbitrator aspires. Unless the parties both see him as someone able to look at the matter without prejudice to one side or the other, then there will be no confidence in his attempt at fairness. This is not only independence from the two parties themselves, but also from extraneous influences such as government policy or sabre-rattling from an interested employer or trade union. It is unrealistic to expect any arbitrator to be immune to influence and devoid of prejudice, but some are seen to be more dispassionate than others. As well as independence the arbitrator needs *authority*. The nature of authority was briefly discussed in chapter 9 and the authority of arbitrators will usually stem from their hierarchical position or their wisdom. The extra quality they may possess is that aforementioned independence, which is not only a detachment from the immediate working situation but also the assumption of experience in other organisations of other problems. In judicial proceedings, in civil and other courts, the judge has his authority shored up by a series of small methods: he wears a distinctive costume, sits both apart from and above other participants in the proceedings, is addressed deferentially and requires everyone to stand when he enters or leaves the room. This is to emphasise the authority traditionally vested in the role. The arbitrator in an industrial dispute or office disagreement does not have all those trappings of authority, but is usually kept at a comfortable distance, both physically and socially, from other participants.

The other two roles are those of *complainant* and *respondent*. They are so similar that the distinction is in many cases only theoretical, but there is a working assumption implied in those terms that one party is complaining about the action or inaction of someone else. It may be a union official complaining about the unacceptable new shift-working system that the management are proposing to introduce or the inadequate pattern of pay differentials. In more formal situations of disagreement between individuals the complainant/respondent roles are less clear, but still help to provide a framework for running the encounter, especially in deciding who starts. As with disciplinary encounters there is a small possibility of additional roles: either witnesses or advocates, but the essential structure is the triangle of arbitrator, complainant and respondent.

(c) Briefing

The arbitrator will brief himself before the encounter with as much information about the matter as he can. This will vary from the one extreme in which he has a hurried telephone conversation while two people fume outside his office, having just had a blazing row, to the other extreme where the arbitrator has detailed written statements of case from both parties beforehand, possibly embroidered by press comment or other background "noise".

(d) Objectives

The arbitrator will set himself some objectives from a reading of the papers or other preliminary information, depending upon what seems to be feasible and without prejudging the issue. He will have the more general objective of "genuinely trying to search for a solution that is likely to be acceptable to both sides" (McCarthy and Ellis, 1973, p. 142) so that not only is there a resolution of the particular issues which is dividing the parties, but also the working relationship between them is at least partially repaired.

Linda Dickens (1979) provides a comment on the range of objectives available to third party interventions in collective matters:

> It may be that the third party will seek to secure what he considers a 'just' or 'equitable' solution. On the other hand, he may take no interest in the form of the settlement – any settlement will do if the parties agree to it, regardless of the merits of each side's position. This latter approach is the one which appears to characterize ACAS conciliation in such cases as unfair dismissal. The third party may look beyond the immediate dispute and attempt to lay the foundations for better relationships in the future. (Dickens, 1979, p. 302)

12.1.2 Encounter

(a) Setting

The setting of the encounter has to express the arbitrator's neutrality. This means ideally that it is not on the "territory" of either the complainant or the respondent, unless there is a clear imbalance in power of the two parties at the outset, in which case a location favouring the weaker party might help to redress that imbalance and enhance the likelihood of a satisfactory outcome.

The formality of the setting will vary with the nature of the encounter, perhaps even the stage of the encounter. Walton (1969, p. 118) describes a mediated encounter between a personnel manager and a production superintendent that began in an office and later moved to a cocktail lounge and on again to a dining room:

> In the office setting there is a greater sense of urgency to get on with whatever one is doing. This is helpful in identifying many of the conflicting views and feelings in a short period of time. By shifting to the restaurant and by adding one round of drinks, the interaction could become somewhat more relaxed, allowing for a mixture of social banter and direct work on the relationship. This sort of mixture often facilitates the more integrative and educative work which must follow the identification and clarification of the issues. (Walton, 1969, p. 118)

In most cases the encounter will be fairly formal, even if it is only to

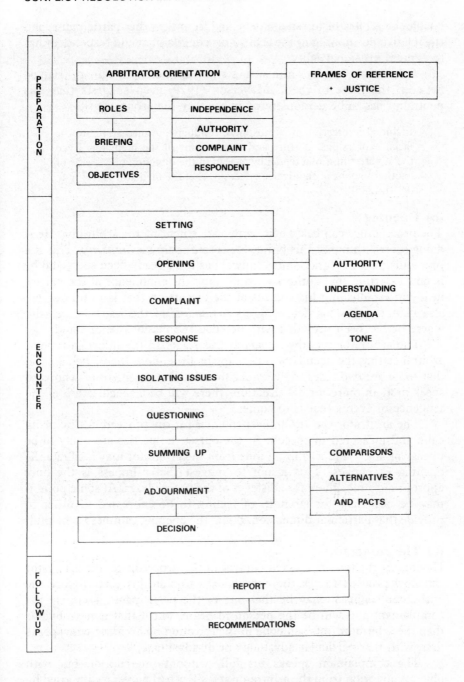

Fig. 12.1   A structured approach to arbitration.

enable the arbitrator to remain detached from the other participants, and the relative positioning of the arbitrator, complainant and respondent has to express his impartiality.

This mainly involves him sitting at the apex of an imaginary triangle between the three of them. Mayerson (1979) even suggests that this neutrality has to be demonstrated in the way the arbitrator sits:

> Included in creating an atmosphere conducive to mediation are the facial expressions, posture and mannerisms of the mediator. Even the slightest hint of a tendency to lean in the direction of one side or another may have an adverse effect on what the mediator is trying to do. (p. 235)

(b) Opening

The proceedings can best begin with a statement by the arbitrator. He is doing several things at this point. He is setting up his *authority*. This is a prerequisite of his functioning anyway, as has already been seen, and he is now asserting that authority, confirming the confidence of the parties in it and establishing his control of the discussion that is to follow. He also demonstrates his degree of *understanding* of the issues, especially where he has been provided with detailed submissions beforehand.

The arbitrator sets the *agenda* at this stage. In the informal type of arbitral setting the agenda will perhaps be little more than a declaration that there are two sides to every argument and a statement of who is to speak first. In more formal situations there will be a specification of the sequence of events that is to come.

The arbitrator can try and set the *tone* for the proceedings by being calm and measured in speech. At the outset the parties are likely to be uneasy or angry and a calming tone from the arbitrator may facilitate the opening exchanges. This is not to suggest that calmness is the only appropriate atmosphere for all stages of the proceedings. At some point it may be necessary for strength of feeling to be expressed in order to provide that particular dimension, but at the opening calmness is helpful.

(c) The complaint

Having set the tone and taken control of the proceedings, the arbitrator can now proceed to ask the complainant to state his case. Before the encounter begins it may be that one of the participants is clearly the complainant and will be the person to begin, but if that is not obvious then the arbitrator puts someone in that position by deciding who speaks first, with that particular advantage or disadvantage.

The complainant speaks his full, without interruption but with obvious attention from the arbitrator and silence (if necessary imposed by the arbitrator) from the respondent. The possible intervention from the arbitrator is questions to clarify or enlarge on some matter that is obvious to the complainant, looking through his particular frame of reference, yet not clear to the arbitrator with less detailed knowledge. *Clarification* is mainly by direct questions (see p. 49) either for information or for precision. An example of a direct question for information would be:

> Complainant: "This is the second time this has happened since Christmas."
> Arbitrator: "What happened last time."

Questioning for precision is usually needed when the complainant is not willing to commit himself to a clear statement, without which the complaint lacks substance:

> Complainant: "All my experience tells me that companies tend to take on commitments that are beyond their means."
> Arbitrator: "Are you saying that this company is taking on commitments that it has not the resources to handle?"

When the statement of the complaint is complete the arbitrator will recapitulate what has been said in brief summary. This recapitulation is one of the main ways in which the arbitrator improves or supports the communication between the parties and is similar to the technique of *reflection*, mentioned on p. 51. Partly he is translating what has been said, where the complainant cannot make his meaning clear, or is reluctant to be precise, and partly he is summarising to show his own understanding to the complainant. He does not turn at once to the respondent and say, "What he means . . ." or "What he is trying to say . . .", as that is assuming the understanding without having confirmed it. The process of recapitulation is *to* the complainant, asking for his confirmation, in the hearing of the respondent. The complainant can correct or add to the recapitulation by the arbitrator until he accepts the version that is now being described. All his exchanges are with the impartial arbitrator rather than with the respondent, whose questions might be regarded as traps.

(d) The response
We now move to a similar statement, but from the respondent. This leaves out the stage, that is normal in legal proceedings, of cross-examination, wherein the respondent would ask questions of the complainant about what he has said. Even in relatively formal arbitrations this is not found: the move is directly to a response, which will include some refutation of what the complainant has alleged, some counter-charges and some failure to comment at all.

At the end of the response the arbitrator will again recapitulate, seeking the respondent's acceptance of his summary and taking up the points in the complaint that the respondent has ignored, so that they can either be accepted or refuted. Most of the difficulties will lie in the unanswered criticisms and in the counter-charges.

(e) Isolating issues

After the two opening statements the arbitrator will isolate the issues that divide the parties. There will already be some points of agreement that can be eliminated from further discussion but their existence is a part of the foundation of the rest of the encounter, as the parties will usually have found more common ground than they expected because they have now come together and stopped elaborating their dissatisfaction. However much still divides them they will almost certainly have found some points of disagreement that they did not expect. This is the basis on which they can now move forward, so some emphasis can usefully be given to those points, although it would be a foolish arbitrator who underestimated the significance of the differences that remained and who tried to smooth over real, outstanding difficulties.

The points of disagreement are what have to be tackled and they also have to be brought into focus, filtering out the irrelevancies, platitudes and generalities so as to direct attention at what lies at the heart of the conflict, with complainant and respondent agreeing with the diagnosis. Until the following agenda is agreed, there is no way forward and the arbitrator may well find that his first interpretation is not shared with the participants, requiring him to reassess the diagnosis until he has it agreed. He is not, of course, making any sort of right/wrong judgements between the participants unless the point is reached where one party or the other is declining acceptance of some particular point, despite the fact that the arbitrator has explored it and is satisfied that it is "true". In that case he has to test his authority by asserting that this is the basis on which he has to proceed.

(f) Questioning

Now the arbitrator questions the parties about the points on which their stories diverge, so as to face them both with the contradictions and produce a clearer idea *in their minds* of why they differ. The questions are phrased to direct attention to difficulties or obscurities without at any time impugning the integrity or objectives of the person being questioned. Questioning can switch quite quickly from complainant to respondent and back again to face them with the inconsistencies and perhaps enable them to see each other's point of view more clearly.

At some stage during this process there is the possibility that the problem will resolve itself. The parties will come to see the other point of view more clearly and may see their way through to a resolution without losing face. If this seems possible the arbitrator may encourage them to exchange directly with each other, abandoning the formality of the enforced triangular exchange. He needs to be reasonably confident that it will succeed, because he is abandoning control.

If the matter is fully ventilated in as calm an atmosphere as possible, between antagonists of equally balanced power, settlement at this stage by this means is a likely outcome with the cold light of reason shone on the mistrust.

(g) Summing up

Although the matter may resolve itself at the questioning stage, it may be a more difficult issue needing a further contribution from the arbitrator, either because the parties lack confidence in their own ability to see the right answer or because one lacks trust in the other. In management/union encounters, for instance, union representatives may feel that they do not understand fully enough the technical aspects of proposed changes in a pay structure and would look to the arbitrator to provide that sort of expertise.

At this stage the arbitrator is making a quite fresh contribution to the discussions, as he is introducing his own interpretation and some of his own suggestions about how the issue can be resolved or accommodated.

First of all he will make *comparisons* between the two interpretations that have been presented during the encounter. This is largely a reiteration of what has been done earlier at the end of the complaint and the response in isolating issues, but it now comes at a different point of the proceedings and in the context of the two additional contributions the arbitrator can now make: fresh *alternatives* and *pacts*. Because the complainant and respondent are so bound up with their own views, they can only see limited alternatives. The arbitrator is less hampered by personal involvement and will see possibilities that the others can not, partly because of his detachment and partly because of the expertise he is able to impart into the discussion as a result of the knowledge he has of other situations. A pact is a particular form of alternative, whereby one party wants something of the other, and he will only obtain it if he provides something in exchange. Mayerson (1979, pp. 243–245) provides a neat example of this in her account of what she calls trade-offs. The arbitrator may, for example, suggest that a union claim that inspectors should receive a premium rate of pay, against management determination to maintain a uniform rate, might be considered more positively by the management if the number of inspectors could be agreed. The arbitrator moves with care in selecting pacts and other alternatives to propose as he is still trying to manoeuvre the parties into making their own agreement. If he moves too far towards one party or the other, he may make that outcome less likely.

(h) Adjournment

In a complex case there will probably be one or more adjournments, as in negotiations, for everyone to reflect on their case while they are having a cup of tea and a rest, but there is a useful place for a "tactical" adjournment after the arbitrator's summing up to allow time for the matter to be reassessed. Complainant and respondent will now see how the arbitrator's mind is working and will have some specific alternatives to consider. Things have moved a long way since the encounter began. There will be a new understanding and information, as well as – perhaps – new misunderstandings, so the parties are now working to a different scenario and have a better chance of making their own settlement. If they can manage that, it will be a much better arrangement than if they wait for the arbitrator to produce his solution, as they will be committing themselves voluntarily to an arrangement that they believe will work.

(i) Decision

The last resort is where the arbitrator tells the parties what to do. In unequivocal, yes/no problems this may be satisfactory, but in the typical wide-ranging, involved matters that only get to arbitration because they are so difficult, an externally imposed resolution can be inadequate. The arbitrator is, however, left with no choice. In the end he has to propound a remedy, if the parties are unable or unwilling to find their own.

12.1.3 Follow-up

(a) Report

The report of the arbitrator will contain the judgement and the main parts of the summing up to explain and justify the decision that the arbitrator has made. Sometimes the decision is first conveyed to the parties in this way. The value of this document goes beyond simply saying what the decision is. It provides the parties with an objective statement about the matter. This will enable them to reflect on how the situation arose and how it might have been averted. It also provides a reference point for both sides in deciding whether the matter has later been resolved in the way that was laid down by the arbitrator.

(b) Recommendations
One of the aspects of the arbitrator's authority is that he walks away once his job is done. For this reason he may be asked to make general recommendations about matters surrounding the disputed question. Some arbitrators would feel that they can only do this if they make the recommendations to both parties rather than just to one; otherwise they would compromise the impartiality that was the basis of the decision they have offered.

References

ACAS *Industrial Relations Handbook*, HMSO, London, 1980.

Dickens, L., "Conciliation, mediation and arbitration in Britain", in Stephenson, G. M. and Brotherton, C. J. (eds.), *Industrial Relations: A Social Psychological Approach*, John Wiley, Chichester, 1979.

Margerison, C. J. and Leary, M., *Managing Industrial Conflicts*, MCB Books, Bradford, 1975.

Mayerson, E. N., *Shoptalk*, Saunders, Philadelphia, 1979.

McCarthy, W. E. J. and Ellis, N. D., *Management by Agreement*, Hutchinson, London, 1973.

Walton, R. E., *Interpersonal Peacemaking*, Addison-Wesley, Reading, Mass., 1969.

PART THREE

SPECIAL CASES AND CONCLUSION

Chapter 13. Interactions with Special Features

Chapter 13

Interactions with Special Features

The classification used in the book does not enable us to put all the inter-actions of organisational life into one of the twelve categories that has been set forth. Some important types of encounter fall outside the classi-fication and need separate treatment. Committees and the less common activity of brainstorming will be discussed in this chapter, followed by some comments on performance appraisal interviewing which is similar, but not identical, to counselling. Finally there is a comment about telephoning.

13.1 Committees

The committee is the standard form of decision-making in a bureaucracy or role culture. The form varies. The board of directors of a limited liability company is a committee, although the significance of each member's contribution may vary according to whether or not he combines with his board membership a full-time post in the management of the company and the level of voting power he represents at a share-holders' meeting.

Reference has been made earlier to the widespread practice in the public sector of employment for staff appointments to be made by panels or small committees with the aim of preventing nepotism. There are many safety committees, suggestions committees, consultative commit-tees and other versions intended to reach collective decisions, even though individual members may have other concerns as well:

> Committees normally consist of 3–20 members . . . to varying degrees concerned about the task, which consists of solving problems and coming to decisions. They may stand to gain or lose personally; they may have their own ideas about the policy the committee should pursue, and may be committed to the success of the enterprise; they may be representatives of other bodies which elected them to the committee, and feel under obligation or pressure to defend their views. (Argyle, 1969, p. 253)

Committees operate in a formal way. There is invariably a *chairman* and normally *minutes* are kept. These may be drafted by a secretary during and after the meeting, with the draft then modified by the chairman, but eventually they have to be accepted by all members at the next meeting. Although the chairman has considerable scope for determining the way in which *proceedings* are recorded and emphasised, there is less scope for determining *decisions* unless the committee members are remarkably compliant. Before a decision is reached it will be framed with some precision. It may be framed by the chairman in a leading way–"Are we all agreed, then, that we proceed to seek tenders?"–or it may be put to the meeting as a motion from one of the members, seconded by another. In the latter case it will be worded precisely and the wording may be clarified or tidied up before the committee, as a whole, votes on it.

Other aspects of formality are that there is usually an *agenda* of items of business and some rules of *procedure* about who speaks, how voting is conducted, and the method of conducting debate through the chairman so that all remarks are directed to him rather than to other committee members.

Committees are semi-permanent bodies so that they tend to meet at predetermined times at regular intervals. This continuity makes important the issue of the *terms of reference* that the committee has: what it is intended to do, what range of authority it has, how it is to operate and how the membership is to be determined.

The formality of encounters gives the chairman considerable influence over proceedings as well as prescribing his authority in certain ways, and his first move will be to settle the *frequency* of meetings. If the committee is to operate soundly its members have to learn to work together, even if that is not always the same as working harmoniously. Frequent meetings enable individual members to get to know each other's method of operating, establish working relationships and understandings, while practising their main job of functioning as a collective entity. In some cases there is a strong will towards cooperative working and even pride in belonging to the committee which is seen as doing a worthwhile job, although meetings have to be sufficiently frequent to continue the practice of working together, without having to rediscover it afresh every time. Some commentators believe that the cohesion of the committee's work depends upon the chairman enthusing each individual member:

> The chairman should take positive steps to ensure that each committee member believes his task to be worthwhile. Initially this may involve seeing individuals separately to discover what their attitudes are and to persuade them, if necessary, about the importance of the work. It may also entail personal discussions with individual members, outside committee work, to ascertain their current feelings and assure them of the value of their presence. (Sidney, Brown and Argyle, 1973, p. 112)

As with arbitration the committee is dependent upon its chairman for its effectiveness, and chairmanship is in many ways similar to arbitrating, involving a degree of impartiality and acting as referee for the discussion that takes place. The first way in which the chairman exercises his authority in the committee encounter itself is in *introducing* each agenda item, which will be presented by him to the committee with remarks that will influence the way in which committee members approach it. Phrases like, "Perhaps we can just get this item out of the way . . ." or "I suppose this is the most important matter we have to consider this afternoon . . ." will tend to make committee members treat those items in the same way. If he is quite wrong in his assessment of the items and the extent to which other members of the committee share his assumptions, his assessment will be challenged and committee proceedings may be protracted and made less effective.

Secondly, the chairman *recognises* people who contribute to the discussion. In trying to maintain a balance in the contributions he will call on some people to speak but not others. It is unlikely he will shut someone out entirely, but he can help the development of the discussion and the achievement of a consensus or majority view by the sequence in which committee members speak. In most cases this is at random, but a chairman may call upon a bland, conciliatory member to speak at a time when the exchanges are getting overheated, or on a controversial, provocative member at a time when the discussion was losing its way and getting bogged down. This requires not only skill but also a shrewd knowledge of what the individual committee members can do. All through proceedings the chairman provides a sense of *purpose*, moving things along and keeping discussion to the point. This will include frequent raising of questions relating to the topic being reviewed in order to expand the committee's discussion of it. With each agenda item the chairman will *summarise* progress and conclusions, including agreement on what action is to be taken and by whom.

Helpful advice on committees is provided in a book by Edgar Anstey (1965). Andrew du Brin (1974, pp. 196–202) summarises the disadvantages and advantages of committees, together with conditions favouring their use, which he regards as:

   (i)   a committee will work effectively when it has the properties of an effective work group in general: optimum size and mix of membership, emotional support for all members, trust and confidence, and an appropriate system of rewards;
  (ii)   a chairman needs to be directive and task oriented in his behaviour, but not necessarily authoritarian;
 (iii)   a chairman will encourage constructive ideas if he shares power and collaborates with members;

(iv) committee members should be technically and personally qualified to be members of the committee and be interested in serving on it.

In the end, committees produce decisions, even though some participants may feel that the process is a tedious and ineffective decision-making method. How can committee decisions be well founded and constructive? The following list is based on suggestions by Locke (1980, p. 167):

Legitimacy. Committee members and other bodies accept the authority of the committee to make the decision, so that any opposition or disagreement will be based on the quality of the decision itself rather than the right of the committee to make it.

Action. The decision should lead to some action, even if it is only settling an argument or agreeing to do nothing.

Soundness. A decision should be taken only after hearing the best advice available and taking care that it fits both the facts of the current situation being considered and any relevant policies or precedents. Any decision which is a break with tradition should include an assessment of the implications of such a departure.

Feasibility. It should be possible for the decision to be translated into action: there is no value in making a decision that is beyond the capability of the organisation to implement.

Timing. This is similar to the point made about in discussing bargaining strategy. Decisions have to be taken at the time that is propitious. If there is no urgency there is no incentive to bottom the issue; if there is no time for discussion, the decision will be hasty and ill-informed. Also some actions require decisions long before implementation.

13.2 Informal Groups

The amount of writing about the working of small informal groups is certainly much greater than the use of such groups in organisational life warrants. This is not only due to the academic interest in such activities, but also because of the belief that some tasks are better undertaken by groups than by individuals. Blau and Scott (1963) list the main reasons for this view:

(a) The sifting of suggestions in social interaction serves as an error-correction mechanism.

(b) The social support furnished in interaction facilitates thinking.
(c) The competition among members for respect mobilizes their energies for contributing to the task.

It has been pointed out by many researchers that the apparent effectiveness in performance may disappear when one considers the number of man-hours that are involved: if one person can solve a problem in six hours it may be more cost-effective than five people solving the same problem in two. That criticism takes no account of either speed or implementation. If a matter is urgent, like correcting a fault in a spacecraft, a solution in two hours will be better than one in six, no matter how many people are involved. Also it is one thing to solve a problem, but another to implement the solution. If those involved in putting a decision into practice take part in making the decision they will be better able to make it work as there will be fewer queries for them to raise: they have been through the whole ratiocination needed already. Also they will be committed to success, on the grounds that people support that which they have helped to create.

One form of informal group is *brainstorming*:

> . . . groups attempt to create a 'freewheeling' atmosphere where any ideas, however absurd, are recorded. Evaluation of the quality of ideas is strictly excluded and is carried out after the idea-generation phase is complete. [The] view is that the flow of ideas in the group will trigger off further ideas whereas the usual evaluative framework will tend to stifle imagination. This may be because group members are concerned not to appear ridiculous in the eyes of others. (Smith, 1973, p. 69)

Variations of this method are used in many areas of organisational life, where fresh ideas have to be found and creativity is required. Another type is the temporary *task force*, working party or project group, which comes into existence for a short time to tackle a single assignment before being disbanded. Group members are chosen for their particular expertise rather than their rank in the organisation, and their tasks are often to reduce costs or improve quality in one specific area of the operation. Management consultants depend heavily upon this mode of solving clients' problems. This form of group was mentioned in chapter 1 as a growing form of collaboration, requiring the development of interpersonal skill. Du Brin comments:

> Interpersonal skills of a greater magnitude than most people possess may be required in the temporary task force arrangement. Rapport

among strangers has to be built in a truncated period of time. Technically competent but interpersonally unsophisticated individuals fail because they require considerable time to establish trust and confidence with others. (du Brin, 1974, p. 204)

In all informal groups the position of the *leader* is crucial, as it is not defined as clearly as in a committee. Much of the social psychologists' experimentation has been with leaderless groups, in that a leader has not been nominated at the outset, even though various group members make bids for leadership. In less rarefied activities there is usually a nominated leader even though he will seldom be the "great man" that is sometimes described as being the appropriate person to discharge the responsibilities. The research on leaderless groups has demonstrated that groups left to their own devices tend to throw up two different types of leader — the task specialist and the social/emotional specialist — both of whom are needed at different times in the group processes (see, for instance, Bales, 1950 & 1958). The first tends to drive the group members to produce ideas and attack the task, while the second produces emotional support for group members whose ideas are derided and rewards for those who are making the significant contributions at the different stages of the discussion. When a group is being formed it may therefore be wise to ensure that both types of capacity are present among the members.

The *size* of the group will influence group effectiveness, according to the task. The larger the group the greater the problems of coordination. Most observers, and those experienced in leading groups, agree that five is the best number. Hare (1962) justified this number on the grounds that an odd number of group members averted the possibility of deadlock, a single group member could be in a minority without the same pressure to conform with the majority that would exist in a smaller group, and there are enough people for members to shift roles easily. If the group task requires little coordination the size could increase, as may be needed for complex tasks, but for urgent matters there may be a base for reducing numbers.

The *mix* of group members may be heterogeneous or homogeneous. Heterogeneous composition is better for complex tasks requiring a diversity of opinion and expertise, and they are also preferred for creative tasks. Where it is very important that the decision made is accurate, there is again a preference for a heterogeneous composition as the diversity of view will ensure a rigorous analysis. Homogeneous groups are better for sequential, interdependent tasks as a chain is no stronger than its weakest link. Homogeneity is also preferred where the required level of cooperation is high or where the task is simple (Bass, 1965).

13.3 Performance Appraisal

Performance appraisal interviewing defies classification by the method used in this book, as it is likely to use all the different styles described. The performance review is a notoriously difficult and unpopular interview, and many management development schemes have foundered through being based on a manager/subordinate discussion that managers refused to conduct or conducted only artificially. The managerial unwillingness can be largely attributed to the sheer difficulty of the job the manager is being asked to do. The subordinate is hoping for good news and apprehensive at the prospect of adverse criticism, although he may also be looking forward to the opportunity of getting some attention to his problems and frustrations. The manager has little to gain personally from the interview, and will be reluctant to criticise in case the response to the criticisms is to shift the responsibility for action back to the manager. He will also want to maintain an equable relationship with the subordinate. Most performance appraisal interviews follow the general pattern of counselling, set out in chapter 9, but the classic account of this type of encounter is by Norman Maier (1958). More recent work is by Anstey et al. (1976) and Randell and his colleagues (1972) produced a book that was of special interest through being set in the context of a single organisation.

13.4 Telephoning

Talking via the telephone presents both problems and opportunities. The first problem is that *non-verbal cues are eliminated*. Deflection of gaze, gesture, blushing and all the other indicators have no communicative effect. Associated with that is the greater importance attached to *the voice*. The listener will make judgements about the speaker on the basis of what the voice sounds like. This is always a component of the mutual assessment between strangers on first meeting, but it has-heightened emphasis in telephoning due to the absence of other cues. A third difficulty is the increase in *simultaneous talking*, which is not as obvious until you think about it. In face-to-face conversation there is little simultaneous speech as one party either waits for the other to finish or is, in some way, waved down by the other if he tries to interrupt. On the telephone the battery of synchronising behaviours is so reduced that there is more simultaneous speech, meaning that less is heard from the other. This is explained not only by the lack of non-verbal cues, but also by the tendency to be distracted by what we *see* during the conversation. In turn this produces an odd inefficiency in telephone conversations, which may take longer than they would face-to-face.

Apart from the extra time that is consumed by telephoning, it is an expensive activity, so that there is always interest in making telephoning more efficient.

The one who answers the telephone speaks first, but what does he say? The answer, "Hello", provides no information other than that there is someone there. The respondent who announces who he is, gets the conversation off to a brisk start. The caller then announces his own identity and leads into the conversation. The exchanges need to be more succinct than in normal conversation, because of the lack of any medium other than speech to convey the message and, for the same reason, there need to be regular pauses for feedback and confirmation that the message is being received and understood. The listener tends to replace the face-to-face smiles and nods with an above-average number of grunts and yesses.

13.5 Conclusion

As this book comes to its close we can look back on the breadth of inter-actions which we have examined and the different sources of explanation we have considered in working out a series of Procrustean beds on which to stretch that most individual of human activities – talking. It is to be hoped that the reader has found in these pages some means of better understanding the exchanges in which he takes part, and some help in making his participation in them more effective.

A large part of the management role in organisations is to maintain an effective system of interpersonal relationships so as to integrate the diverse activities of those working in the organisation, focussing their efforts towards common goals. Although organisational structures play a large part in this process, the manager's ability to handle a range of interactive episodes with a variety of other people is the key factor in communicative success. This requires from managers not only greater understanding and the development of personal effectiveness: it also requires action.

Implicit in the managerial role as boundary spanner or liaison is the need to transcend structural barriers that impede the flow of communication in an organization. The manager who does not or cannot maintain an effective network of interpersonal communication relationships will become a victim of executive isolation. To avoid isolation, managers must take the initiative in establishing direct communication with their subordinates. Walking out into work areas and inviting employees into the manager's office are more likely to generate effective communication than a traditional open-door policy, which requires the subordinate to take the first step. (Baskin and Aronoff, 1980, p. 160)

The material of this book does not relate only to interactive "set pieces" but to all the communications activity of organisational life, each incident of which will follow one or more of the patterns described. Managers need not only to respond, but also to initiate.

The final comment is to remind everyone that style without substance is dangerous. This can be illustrated by another literary allusion.

Hamlet's uncle, the King, is so full of anguish about his brother's murder ("O my offence is rank, it smells to Heaven . . .") that he seeks to expiate his guilt in prayer but has to abandon the attempt because his heart is not in it:

"My words fly up, my thoughts remain below.
Words without thoughts never to Heaven go."

The most carefully orchestrated speech or painstaking counselling interview is unsuccessful if it is mere words. We need not only words, and a way with words, but also words that carry thoughts which match the words and are right for the situation in which they are uttered. The following anecdote shows the importance of both the message and the source.

A company was introducing a new pension scheme and one of the terms was that all employees should join. The only person who would not take part was Fred, who had been there since time immemorial. The Personnel Manager, Works Convenor and Works Director all tried to persuade Fred to change his mind but failed. The Company Chairman heard about the difficulty and called Fred into his office:

Chairman: "Fred, sign here or you're fired."
Fred: "Yes sir, right away, sir."
Chairman: "If you sign so readily when I ask you, why didn't you sign before?"
Fred: "Ah well, no-one else explained it properly."

References

Argyle, M., *Social Interaction*, Tavistock Publications, London, 1969.

Anstey, E., *Committees: How They Work and How to Work Them*, Allen & Unwin, London, 1965.

Anstey, E., Fletcher, C. A. and Walker, J., *Staff Appraisal and Development*, Allen & Unwin, London, 1976.

Bales, R. F., *Interaction Process Analysis*, Addison-Wesley, Cambridge, Mass., 1950.

Bales, R. F., "Task roles and social roles in problem-solving groups", in Maccoby, E. E. *et al.* (eds.), *Readings in Social Psychology*, Holt, Rinehart & Winston, New York, 1958.

Baskin, A. W. and Aronoff, C. E., *Interpersonal Communication in Organizations*, Goodyear Publishing Co., Santa Monica, Calif., 1980, p. 160.

Bass, B. M., *Organisation Psychology*, Allyn & Bacon, Boston, 1965.

Blau, P. M. and Scott, W. R., "Processes of communication in formal organizations" (1963), in Argyle, M. (ed.), *Social Encounters*, Penguin, Harmondsworth, 1976.

du Brin, A. J., *Fundamentals of Organizational Behavior*, Pergamon Press, New York, 1974.

Hare, P. A., *Handbook of Small Group Research*, Free Press, New York, 1962.

Locke, M., *How to Run Committees and Meetings*, Macmillan, London, 1980.

Maier, N. R. F., *The Appraisal Interview*, Wiley, New York, 1958.

Randell, G., Shaw, R., Packard, P. and Slater, J., *Staff Appraisal*, Institute of Personnel Management, London, 1972.

Sidney, E., Brown, M. and Argyle, M., *Skills with People*, Hutchinson, London, 1973.

Smith, P. B., *Groups within Organizations*, Harper & Row, London, 1973.

Index